Visual
Tennis

T E N

DOUBLEDAY

New York   London   Toronto   Sydney   Auckland

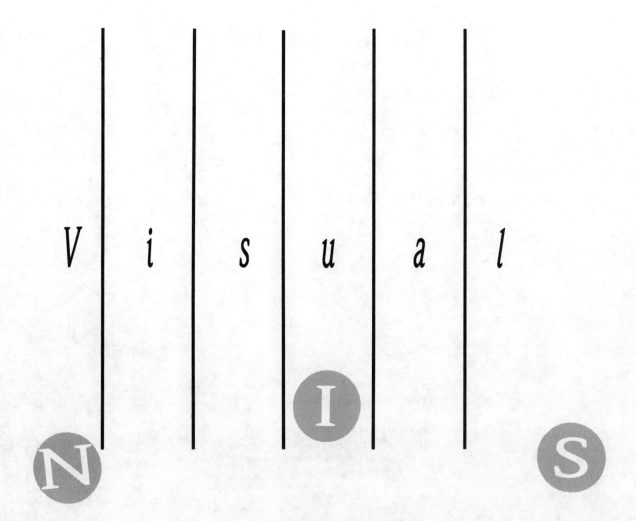

Visual TENNIS

Mental Imagery and the Quest for the Winning Edge

John Yandell

Foreword by Dick Gould
Photographs by Julie Polunsky

To Cynnie and Bud

PUBLISHED BY DOUBLEDAY
a division of Bantam Doubleday Dell Publishing Group, Inc.
666 Fifth Avenue, New York, New York 10103

DOUBLEDAY and the portrayal of an anchor
with a dolphin are trademarks of Doubleday,
a division of Bantam Doubleday Dell
Publishing Group, Inc.

Library of Congress Cataloging-in-Publication Data
Yandell, John.
Visual tennis : mental imagery and the quest for the winning
edge / John Yandell. — 1st ed.
p.   cm.
1. Tennis—Psychological aspects.   2. Imagery (Psychology)
3. Visualization.   I. Title.   II. Title: Visual tennis.
GV1002.9.P75Y36   1990
796.342′01′9—dc20   89-28339
                                                          CIP

ISBN 0-385-26422-4
Copyright © 1990 by John Yandell
with photos by Julie Polunsky

Acknowledgments

It is a pleasure to acknowledge the people who have helped me in the development of the teaching system presented here. The list begins with my first tennis coach Frank Ward, who later also taught me to be a teacher, and with Bill Austin, one of the most charismatic pros I have known, who taught me to hit a backhand in one hour.

There are the numerous individuals in the Bay Area tennis community who have given me knowledge, support, and critical feedback over the years. The debt my work owes to Dick Gould is acknowledged in the text. I want to thank him personally for sharing his time and his encouragement with me so freely. Alan Davis requires recognition for giving me my first head pro job at Golden Gate Park. Without his confidence in me this book would never have been written.

I want to thank other tennis comrades. Scott Murphy, practice partner, and coaching adversary, has read parts of this book at various stages, as have Charlie Hoeveler, director of the Adidas Tennis Camps, and Weston Reese, director of tennis at the San Francisco Tennis Club. Their enthusiasm and comments have been valued. Fellow teaching pros Michael Friedman and Julie Montague have helped me, not only by reading the text, but by testing the techniques presented here on the teaching court with hundreds of tennis players. My friend Peter Pearson, a beautiful technical player and the source of many of my own spontaneous visual learning experiences, has provided continuous support and entertaining commentary throughout the course of the project.

Christine Guarnaccia of the International Tennis Hall of Fame has been an important source for video and written material on the history of the game's styles. My student Cliff West, in addition to subjecting himself to numerous experiments in teaching theory, introduced me to the joys, and occasional agonies, of modern word processing.

The photos at the heart of this book's teaching sequences need special comment. First, I want to thank my longtime creative associate Chuck Koton for shooting the test photo sequences. The images you see here are the product of the skill of my photographer, Julie Polunsky, who worked closely with me in what was probably the most intense phase of the project. I also want to thank Marty Takigawa and the other printers at HiFi laboratories in San Francisco for producing the large number of technically demanding prints on a very compressed schedule. I also feel special gratitude to my agent, Angela Miller, who, a long time ago, planted the idea for this book in my mind.

Finally, there is the team at Doubleday that made *Visual Tennis* a reality, starting with my editor, Kara Leverte. I was extremely fortunate to have, in Kara, an editor who not only knew the game of tennis and played it well herself, but someone who understood that there was something new in the concept for this book, and was willing to work at every stage to give it shape and expression. Her assistant, Marirose Ferrara, also made special efforts to facilitate the project. My designer, Carol Malcolm, performed with seeming ease the difficult task of translating a teaching process into words and pictures on printed pages. Finally, I want to acknowledge Patty Moynihan of the Doubleday marketing department, an avid player herself, for her enthusiasm for the book, and her effort to make it accessible to tennis players everywhere.

CONTENTS

Foreword by Dick Gould   3

INTRODUCTION   5

HOW VISUALIZATION WORKS   11

THE CLASSICAL STYLE   17

THE FOREHAND   27

Creating the Forehand Swing Pattern   31
Executing the Forehand   40
Muscle Memory Corrections   42
Keying the Forehand   45
Variation: The Circular Backswing   52
Variation: The Closed Face Backswing   54

THE BACKHAND   57

Creating the One-Handed Topspin
    Backhand Swing Pattern   63
Executing the One-Handed Topspin Backhand   72
Muscle Memory Corrections   74
Keying the One-Handed Topspin Backhand   77
Variation: The One-Handed Slice Backhand   84

Creating the Two-Handed Backhand Swing Pattern   87
Executing the Two-Handed Backhand   96
Muscle Memory Corrections   98
Keying the Two-Handed Backhand   101

THE RELATIONSHIP BETWEEN TIMING AND POWER | 109

THE VOLLEY | 113

Creating the Forehand Volley Swing Pattern | 117
Executing the Forehand Volley | 126
Muscle Memory Corrections | 127
Keying the Forehand Volley | 130
Variation: The Underspin Forehand Volley | 134

Creating the One-Handed Backhand Volley
   Swing Pattern | 137
Executing the One-Handed Backhand Volley | 146
Muscle Memory Corrections | 147
Keying the One-Handed Backhand Volley | 150
Variation: The Underspin Backhand Volley | 154

Creating the Two-Handed Backhand Volley
   Swing Pattern | 157
Executing the Two-Handed Backhand Volley | 166
Muscle Memory Corrections | 167
Keying the Two-Handed Backhand Volley | 170

THE SERVE | 175

Creating the Swing Pattern for the Basic Serve | 181
Executing the Basic Serve | 192
Muscle Memory Corrections | 194
Keying the Basic Serve | 197
Variation: The Advanced Serve | 204

USING YOUR STROKE KEYS ON THE COURT | 208

THE GRIPS | 213

The Forehand Grips | 215
The One-Handed Backhand Grip | 216
The Two-Handed Backhand Grip | 217
The Continental Grip | 218

Foreword

Occasionally, a book comes along that has something genuinely new and exciting to say about the game of tennis. *Visual Tennis: Mental Imagery and the Quest for the Winning Edge* is one of these exceptional books.

In these pages, John Yandell presents us with a new approach to learning and playing the game. *Visual Tennis* is based on the insight, now well documented by research in sports psychology, that sports learning is naturally visual. Tennis players have always learned by watching better players, and often play far above their normal levels after doing so. *Visual Tennis* is a complete teaching system based on visual techniques.

Visual Tennis teaches you to think about your game in a different medium, in images rather than in words. In the individual chapters, Yandell provides what are among the most detailed visual models ever created for all the basic shots: groundstrokes, volleys, and serves. Each stroke is shown in full from both the front and side views, and then broken down into its key components. By mastering the key images, students learn to produce superior strokes effortlessly and automatically. Unlike many instructional books, *Visual Tennis* includes models for both the one-handed and two-handed backhands, and shows you how to decide which is right for you.

Visual Tennis goes beyond teaching basic strokes, however. Perhaps its most important contribution is to show players at all levels how to use visualization to produce their best tennis under the pressure of match play. To do this, Yandell effectively uses a system of stroke keys. By visualizing the key just before hitting a shot, the player triggers the correct execution of the stroke pattern, no matter what the situation on the court.

Of special additional value, Yandell provides an analytic comparison of the three major styles of play: the continental, the western, and the eastern, or classical. He points out the strengths and weaknesses of each, and shows that the classical strokes are the most effective for the majority of players, and also, the easiest to learn. He explains how most of the great modern players use some variation of classical strokes, and why the classical style can be used with equal success for serve and volley, the baseline game, or any combination of the two.

Would you like to play winning "A" tennis at your club? Are you a junior player who would like to move up in the junior rankings, or earn a ranking for the first time? The book states that these goals are realistic for virtually any player. Players who adopt the total visual approach often progress several ability levels, competing against and beating players who had previously seemed out of reach.

Visual Tennis has value for everyone in tennis from the beginner to the ranked tournament player. It will be of special interest to theorists of the game, and to working teaching pros who would like to produce the same results with their own students. In the Introduction, Yandell includes a critical analysis of the failures of the traditional approaches to teaching. He shows how visualization transcends the inherent limitations of most tennis instruction, by creating a teaching technology based on the way athletes actually learn.

With the publication of this book, John Yandell establishes himself as one of the most innovative tennis teachers in the country. His critically acclaimed video *The Winning Edge*, starring John McEnroe and Ivan Lendl, is a best-selling instructional tape, and is widely used by teaching pros and at tennis camps across the country. In *Visual Tennis*, Yandell sets out his theories of visual modeling in greater detail, and provides a fresh set of model stroke patterns for every aspect in the game. The images of the strokes alone make the book worthwhile. But what is more promising is the prospect that every player who uses them as part of the visualization training process has the potential to hit the ball with the same fluidity and technical precision.

I have known John for ten years, since his days as a graduate student in the humanities at Stanford. His work provides a new analytic perspective on the game. This book excites me and is highly recommended to any reader interested in discovering his or her true potential.

—DICK GOULD
MEN'S TENNIS COACH
STANFORD UNIVERSITY

INTRODUCTION

As a tennis player, has this ever happened to you? After watching great tennis, you went out and played the best tennis of your life. The match you saw may have been on television, at a pro tournament, at a club, or the public courts. Afterward, it was as if you could not miss. You had total control of the ball, and effortlessly dominated your opponent. You went to the courts the next time expecting to play the same way, but instead, the effect had disappeared.

What you experienced was the spontaneous power of visual learning. Visual learning is at the root of how great tennis players learn and play the game. Great players do this intuitively, often without consciously realizing how it occurs. The average player, however, needs help to develop this same ability in himself. Unfortunately, this is something he almost never receives, since the traditional approaches to teaching the game are not based on visual learning, and therefore cannot cultivate this powerful natural ability in students. The result is that the majority of players have the kind of tennis experience described above only by accident, if at all.

It's not surprising that by watching other players, you absorb something from them, almost by osmosis. But why does this happen? The answer has to do with the nature of the learning process. In reality, *all* sports learning, tennis included, is essentially visual. Anyone who has learned to throw a baseball or a football, or to shoot a jump shot, can probably recall watching and imitating someone else.

The term that best describes this modeling process is *visualization*. To define it in the words of noted sports psychologist Jim Loehr, "Visualization is thinking in pictures."[1] We learn sports motions naturally, by visualizing images of

[1]James E. Loehr, Mental Toughness Training for Sports: Achieving Athletic Excellence (*Lexington, Mass: Stephen Greene Press, 1986*). *Loehr stresses the importance of visualization training in his overall approach to developing mental toughness. See pp. 105–10.*

them first. These images then become a kind of mental blueprint for the body to follow. The way John McEnroe learned to play tennis is a typical example. As McEnroe describes it, "When I was learning to play, I just watched Rod Laver and tried to do what he did."

Ivan Lendl had a similar experience as a young player. He would play much better after ball-boying matches for the top adult Czechoslovakian players. "Being on the court so close to the players I saw things, and then I would start to do them myself," he said.

Sports psychologists have demonstrated that the ability to visualize is linked to performance in almost every known sport. They have devised training programs using visualization techniques in football, basketball, baseball, track and field, skiing, and golf, to mention a few of the best-known examples. These programs systematically enhance the natural visual learning process. Visualization is now regularly incorporated into the training programs of the world's top athletes.

A recent overview of the scientific literature concluded that visualization is a proven factor in improving sports performance. How powerful? In experiments measuring improvements in sports skills, the overview concluded, visualization *by itself*, that is visualization even *without* physical practice, produced measurable improvement in performance across a wide range of motor skills.[2] If you stop to think about it, this is a rather startling conclusion. The inference is that tennis players can increase their success simply by *thinking correctly* (in pictures) about their sport, independent of practice time on the court. The study concludes that a combination of regular practice and visualization is the key to the development of the athlete's full potential.

Although the effectiveness of visualization has been demonstrated in research, and visualization training has become an established aspect of Olympic and professional sports, this book is among the first programs to make the same training available to recreational and competitive athletes below the world-class level. Its purpose is to set out a teaching technology for tennis that is based on the visual learning process.

In 1985, I collaborated with John McEnroe and Ivan Lendl on the creation of *The Winning Edge*, a tennis video that also made use of the principles of visualization. In the video, McEnroe and Lendl provide visual models for the strokes and shot patterns. First they break the stroke or technique down into its key components. Then they reconstruct the motion into a fluid whole. The viewer, by visualizing as he watches the video, transfers the images into his mental imagery. These images then become the basis for forming his own shots.[3]

This book goes beyond the video in that it not only breaks down each stroke pattern into its component parts, but also offers a detailed series of checkpoints to help the tennis player turn his visual model of each stroke into a more precise physical motion. These checkpoints allow students to evaluate how closely they are following the model on a regular basis, form the basis for doing what are called "muscle memory corrections." The corrections allow any player to correct his mistakes as they actually happen, before they can become permanently ingrained in the stroke pattern. Developed by Stanford tennis coach Dick Gould and his partner Tom Chivington, muscle memory is one of the most powerful techniques ever devised for correcting technical flaws in stroke production. The process is explained in detail for each stroke in the individual chapters.

---

[2]*Deborah L. Feltz and Daniel M. Landers, "The Effects of Mental Practice on Motor Skill Learning and Performance: A Meta-analysis,"* Journal of Sports Psychology, 1983.

---

[3]*A pioneering video in the field is* Tennis with Stan Smith *from Sybervision. The Sybervision theory is that, at least occasionally, every player hits the ball correctly. By watching the video the player is supposed to bring out this preexisting muscle memory. In reality, developing consistent stroke patterns requires a more detailed and systematic approach. Since the strokes are not broken down into their component parts, it is difficult to use the tape to form clear visual models. Many viewers also find the continuous repetition of the same images difficult to watch. However, Stan Smith's strokes are without doubt a source for many solid technical models, and I recommend the tape for the supplemental video training outlined here.*

Finally, *Visual Tennis* goes beyond the video in offering powerful techniques that can be used to produce consistent strokes under match play conditions. Each chapter provides a series of selected images or "stroke keys" that the player uses to trigger the correct technical stroke pattern. Working with the keys, a player can create his own stroke key chart for every shot. These keys provide any player with the avenue for achieving consistent stroke production, even under competitive pressure.

Currently, tennis instruction can be almost universally divided into two basic schools of thought, neither of which utilizes visual learning in a systematic way. The first, and the most dominant, is the "tennis tip" school. This school teaches the game through a series of self-contained "tips" about various aspects of the game. A common tip from this school is, for example, "Start low and finish high on your groundstrokes," or "Take a short backswing on the volley."

Perhaps you've taken lessons, or seen other players taking lessons, in which the pro offers an array of tips such as these, yet none of them seem to have a positive impact on the stroke. Trying to prepare early, for example, the student jerks the racket back, but every backswing is slightly different, and the rhythm of the motion is destroyed. Next the student tightens up his arm trying to keep a firm wrist, but this makes the contact late and jarring. He tries whipping his body through the ball at various times, but the shots are uncontrolled, and the pace fluctuates wildly. He experiments with a variety of different follow-throughs, but none of them seem to influence where the ball lands. Meanwhile, the pro constantly feeds the student more information, tries to be encouraging, but secretly wonders why teaching a basic stroke is so difficult. If this is all you have seen or experienced, then you have no way of understanding that learning to hit the tennis ball does *not* have to involve this kind of frustration.

To be fair, the leading exponents of this school have done significant research into the biomechanics of the game, and, in fact, some of their most important conclusions are cited here. Their failure has been in translating the raw data into a truly effective teaching technology. Simply put, their approach to teaching starts with the false assumption that verbal commands, or "tips," can be used successfully to teach physical motions. The truth is that they can't. In the typical lesson situation described above, the student attempts to apply a tip such as "keep your wrist firm" to his forehand. But the focus on a verbal message leads to a mechanical response and the isolation of one set of muscles, with no concept of how the "tip" relates to the stroke as a whole. When the student is unsuccessful in improving the stroke, he usually ends up blaming himself for his lack of progress and concludes that he simply lacks the ability to hit the ball well. Many teaching pros go through the course of their careers thinking that the situation described above is normal, and never question the ineffectiveness of the tennis tip method.

But other teaching pros have reacted to this experience in a different way. Rather than simply accept the futility of the tennis tip method, they have rejected it altogether in favor of a second teaching approach, what I call the "mystical" school. The mystical school responds to the inadequacy of verbal instruction by abandoning tips and analysis altogether. Instead, it focuses on the so-called "inner game," or the internal mental dialogue that occurs when you play tennis.

The mystical school teaches that it is the player's internal dialogue, either about his fears and self-doubts, or about technique that prevents the student from learning to hit the ball. The focus, in the view of the mystical school, should not be inward, but rather turned *outward*, entirely to the ball. The role of the instructor is to help students reach a kind of "mystical union" with the ball.

According to the extreme version of this school, by watching the ball, and doing literally nothing else, anyone can develop excellent strokes. The human body already "knows" how to play tennis. The art of teaching is to help the student get the mind out of the way, so that tennis can "happen."

There is no doubt that this approach

contains a powerful truth about the game of tennis, that is, that ball focus is a crucial aspect of learning and playing well. It is also correct in pointing out that verbal commands do not necessarily lead to improved technical stroke production. It correctly identifies the negative role that a player's internal mental dialogue can play in preventing good tennis. It also advocates watching the technique of superior players. But by any objective measure, this approach never leads to the development of solid stroke production for the majority of players. Because it provides no information whatsoever about the bio-mechanics of hitting tennis balls, its results are, on the whole, inferior to even the tennis tip school. The real beneficiaries of the inner game are advanced players who already have well-developed strokes, and who use its insights to improve the mental aspects of their play.[4]

The common problem with both the mystical and the tennis tip approach is that neither one offers a teaching technology based on the process by which sports learning really occurs, that is, by visual assimilation. McEnroe was not the first, or the last, young player to learn by copying great champions. In fact, the rise of various styles of play among junior and recreational players mirrors the changing styles of the players at the top of the professional game. The dominance of Jimmy Connors and Chris Evert in the 1970s established the two-handed backhand as a permanent aspect of the game. Bjorn Borg touched off a movement to heavy topspin and a defensive, baseline style of play. When John McEnroe dethroned Borg, the serve and volley style soared in popularity. This development was paralleled in the women's game by the attacking play of Martina Navratilova. When Ivan Lendl and Boris Becker moved to the top of the tennis world, suddenly the one-handed backhand came back.

There is no point in denying that tennis is a challenging sport. To play good tennis, you must execute a variety of complex physical mo-

tions with consistent precision. The most talented young players do this automatically and unconsciously, but the majority of players lack the exceptional visual learning skill necessary to do this entirely on their own. Instead, they are limited to occasional flashes of brilliance, for example, after watching the superior technique of others. To perform consistently they need help to cultivate the natural, visual learning process. But most teaching pros, despite their sincere intentions and heroic efforts, are unable to provide them that help, because the two predominant schools of instruction are not based on the real nature of sports learning. To the extent that most traditional lessons work, it is because the students either model themselves on the strokes of their teachers, or because they possess the natural ability to translate the verbal information into visual images.

Visual Tennis is based on more than ten years of teaching, coaching, and research. As a teaching pro, I have taught over ten thousand hours of lessons using the principles of visualization training. I have seen it benefit players competing at the professional level, in college, in junior tournaments, in club matches, in club tournaments, and in friendly recreational play.

In addition to my own experiences over the years with spontaneous visual learning, a second factor in the genesis of my approach goes back to the late 1970s, when I was a student at Stanford. During that time I first met men's tennis coach Dick Gould, and learned his teaching system, working as one of his recreational tennis instructors. Dick is known as the legendary coach of ten Stanford men's college championship teams. What is less well publicized is that he also runs one of the largest and most successful instructional programs in the country, teaching players at all levels, from complete beginners to nationally ranked junior players. As far as I know, Dick and his partner, Tom Chivington, the Foothill College tennis coach and the coach of touring pro Brad Gilbert,

---

[4]*See Timothy Gallwey,* The Inner Game of Tennis, *(New York: Random House, 1974), and* Inner Tennis, Playing the Game, *(New York: Random House, 1976). Gallwey's discussion of ball focus was a vital contribution that changed the way the game is understood. The technology of stroke production presented here is compatible with Gallwey's concentration techniques.*

were the first teachers in the country to make explicit stroke models the basis of a teaching system.

Visual Tennis has evolved, in part, from my experience with Gould's sytem. Readers who are familiar with Dick's classic book will recognize the debt my work owes him.[5] My departure is in defining the causal role of the visual dimension in the learning process, and in making it the basis for an entire teaching approach. In a certain way, this visual dimension was latent in Dick's and Tom's concept of a model stroke. In my opinion, the use of physical models worked because they activated the natural visual learning process. However, in my own extensive subsequent teaching, I found the physical models alone were often insufficient to produce consistent stroke production. Eventually, I realized that the model strokes had worked for me because they triggered *mental images* of the correct stroke patterns. The majority of players, however, needed explicit instruction in order to do this for themselves. This insight started the evolution of the visualization training system. In effect I was using Dick's stroke models to create a method that would systematically produce the kind of visual learning experiences I had had spontaneously so many times as a player.

In addition to approaching the game by emphasizing the visual dimension, this book also differs from Dick's approach in the exact form of the model strokes offered. I have altered aspects of the models for the groundstrokes and volleys. I have also created new models for the footwork on the advanced serve. These changes are based on my own teaching experience, my work with McEnroe and Lendl in making *The Winning Edge*, and on the analysis of the stroke patterns of successful players at all levels.

While it is essential to define stroke patterns precisely, what is even more essential is a technology that will turn these patterns into real tennis. In my opinion, the quality of the stroke production in recreational and competitive tennis could be drastically higher than it actually is.

Despite major investments in lessons, clinics, tennis camps, wide-body rackets, etc., far too many players have technical inconsistencies that limit their development and cause them continuous frustration. The inability of most players to improve cannot be blamed on the players themselves, or on the efforts of their instructors. Rather, it lies in the nature of tennis instruction itself.

Of course there are physical differences between players—some have better hand-eye coordination, or are stronger, faster, or more mentally determined. These factors may set some upper limit on a player's development, but frequently, they do not come into play in deciding matches. This is because technique tends to determine the outcome of most matches below the very highest levels of play. But superior technique is something that virtually every player can develop. It is a matter of approaching the game with the right instructional principles, and making the effort to put them into practice.

What kind of results can you achieve using the system presented here? I have found that any club player who follows the principles in this book can learn to compete at the "A" level, and that any junior player can improve a minimum of ten places in the sectional rankings, or achieve a ranking for the first time. Usually this can be accomplished within a period of one year or less, if a player is willing to dedicate himself to the process.

There is a causal relationship between the use of visual images and the proper execution of physical strokes. If you follow the program outlined in this book, you will be able to duplicate the magic that most tennis players experience only by accident. You will learn to play with a classical style that is technically sound, physically effortless, and aesthetically pleasing. You will develop the ability to hit with pace, depth, spin, and precise ball control. In short, you will learn to play the best tennis of your life for the rest of your life.

---

[5]*Dick Gould, Tennis Anyone? 4th ed. (Palo Alto, Calif.: Mayfield, 1988). This book is the best introduction to all aspects of the game ever written.*

9

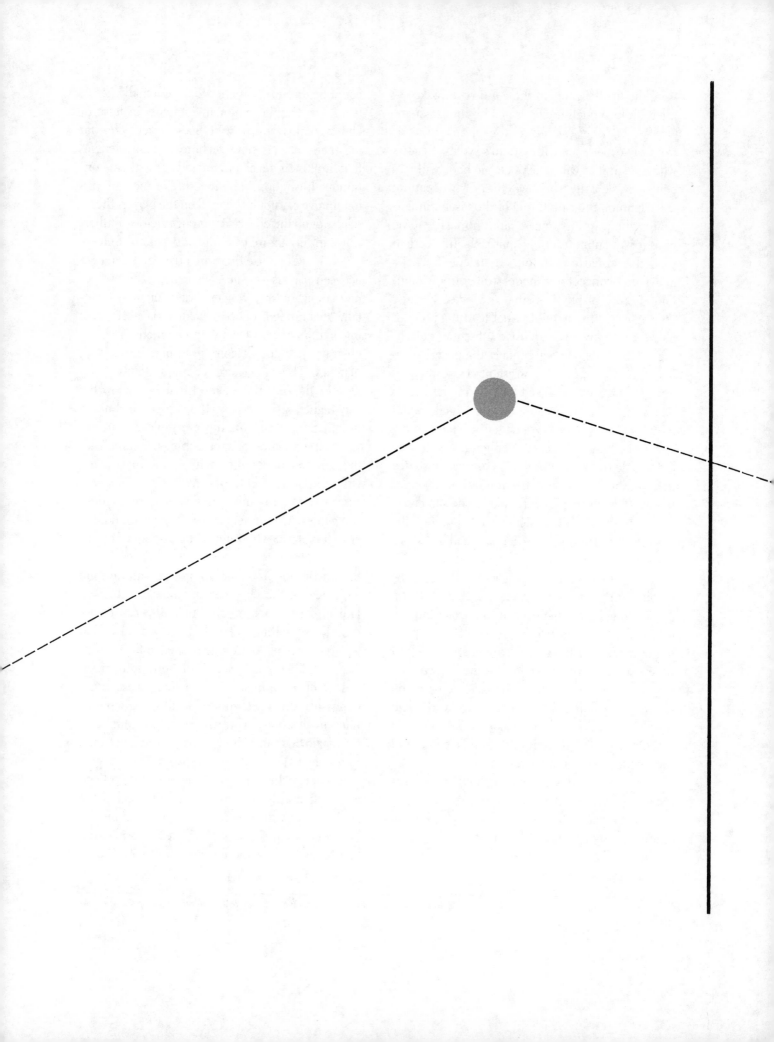

HOW VISUALIZATION WORKS

If you study tennis below the pro level, you will come to the conclusion that the majority of points, and therefore the majority of matches, are lost, rather than won. Specifically, most points are lost on errors, and primarily, on unforced errors. An unforced error means that a player fails to hit the ball over the net and in the court on a basic shot. The error was not forced by pressure from the opponent, it was a breakdown in stroke production on what should have been a routine stroke. A study of club matches showed that, on the average, if the player who lost the match had gotten just one more shot over the net in every point, he would have ended up winning the match instead.

Unforced errors occur for two principle reasons: first, most players have too much variation in their basic stroke technique from ball to ball, and second, they attempt to hit too many shots that are too good, either winners in impossible situations or shots hit with far more velocity than is actually necessary to win the point.

If you watch the top players you will notice they rarely make these kinds of errors. Most points in professional tennis are won, not lost. They are decided by winners or forcing shots, not unforced errors. This is primarily due to the remarkable consistency of these players' stroke patterns. In pro tennis, you see shot after shot executed with unfailing technical precision, despite ball velocities that often exceed 100 miles per hour.

To their credit, club players and junior tournament players often recognize that it is the lack of consistent strokes that causes their errors and limits their performance. They try to correct this through lessons, but, too frequently, without noticeable success. Lessons usually do not produce good stroke technique because the major schools of tennis instruction do not work with the visual learning process.

Visualization training offers the tennis player the opportunity to learn to hit any shot in the game with a high degree of technical precision, and to do so consistently under the pressure of competitive play. Until you have experienced the satisfaction of hitting short balls for winners on a routine basis, or passing down the line consistently on the backhand side, or putting together a series of dominating serve and volley points, you cannot truly appreciate visualization training's power and value.

The chapters that follow outline an approach for hitting all the basic shots: the groundstrokes, the volleys, and the serve. In the backhand chapter, there are sections on hitting with one hand or two, as well as a discussion of how to determine which stroke you should develop. The chapters are designed to be used together, or independently, so that a player can work on one or more individual strokes.

Each chapter begins by providing the player with a *model stroke*. This model has both a *visual* and a *physical* component. To learn a given stroke it is necessary to master both the visual and the physical aspects of the model. This means learning to visualize a technically perfect stroke, and at the same time, to swing the racket according to the image. The role of the visual model is crucial for one simple reason: if you cannot *see* youself swing the racket correctly in your own mind, you will be unable to swing it correctly on the court. Learning a clear mental model gives the body the information it needs to hit the shot, and to hit it the same way on every ball.

In each chapter, you will learn to master the visual and physical models simultaneously. To do this, the strokes will first be broken down into several component parts, what I call the "still frames." By putting the four still frames together, the player learns to execute the swing physically. Simultaneously, he learns to visualize the swing in his mind's eye. The goal is for the two models to correspond as precisely as possible.

At first, this procedure of dividing the strokes into still frames and checkpoints may seem somewhat complex and difficult to learn. Actually, in the long run, the opposite is true. It may sound simpler just to say "Swing low to high on the forehand," and leave it at that, but what does a statement like this really mean? The racket can be in at least four or five different positions on the turn, all of which could be considered "low." But which one, if any, will be correct? Where exactly, does the racket head point? How far back does it go? What position is the arm in? Where are the shoulders and legs?

The purpose of the still frames and the checkpoints is to define exactly where the body and racket are positioned at each stage of the stroke. In the long run this will lead to simplicity, not confusion. The goal is to use the checkpoints to learn what the correct positions actually feel like physically, and more importantly, what they *look* like in the mind's eye. This is done through a series of successive, gradual approximations, working with the checkpoints until the model stroke pattern becomes natural. The goal is not to instantly memorize a long list of information about each stroke, but rather to create deep muscle memory of excellent technical stroke patterns. The checkpoints are only guides to help you see and feel what correct stroke patterns are really like. Used correctly, what you should remember is not only the checkpoints themselves, but the feeling and the image of what the stroke is like when the checkpoints are correct. If you take the time to work with the checkpoints until they are comfortable—it will more than pay off in the quality of your tennis.

After learning the still frames and putting them together into practice swings, the second aspect of developing the model stroke is hitting balls in what is called *controlled drill*. A basic principle of visualization training is that it is *literally impossible* to learn or correct stroke patterns in competitive play, or even in a normal rally. Controlled drill means that the player uses either a partner, a teaching pro, or, if possible, a ball machine to feed him practice balls. At first, the balls should be hit *with low to moderate pace*. They should also come directly to the player, allowing him to execute the stroke *without* having to move. Working in controlled drill allows the player to concentrate entirely on the correct execution of the stroke and the development of his visualization skills.

The controlled drill is also critical because it allows the player to learn the process of *muscle memory correction*. Muscle memory corrections are a central part of the visualization learning process, because they allow a player to correct his mistakes *literally as they happen*. To do a muscle memory correction, the player learns to freeze at the end of a given stroke in what is known as the "statueman" (or "statuewoman") position. By freezing in the statueman position, the player can carefully evaluate the accuracy of the stroke pattern. He does this by comparing his *actual* finish position to the checkpoints for the model stroke. The player than makes a *muscle memory correction* by physically adjusting from his statueman position to the correct position.

Muscle memory work is one of the most powerful aspects of the visualization process. Doing muscle memory corrections eliminates a primary failure in traditional lessons. This occurs when the student makes a technical mistake, and then without correcting, simply recovers to the ready position. The pro points out the error, but the student makes the same error on the next ball, or often makes a new error trying to correct the old error. This pattern can repeat itself to the point of absurdity: the pro gives the same tip over and over, the player goes back and forth from one error to another, but no fundamental change occurs. Muscle memory correction gives the tennis player—and the teaching pro—a way to break this unproductive cycle. It is the only technique that gives the player a physical demonstration of how far his stroke deviated from the correct pattern, and what it actually takes to correct the error.

An indispensable part of developing your strokes and learning the muscle memory cor-

rection process is seeing your tennis on video. You can accomplish this by using a home video camera, or better, by working with a pro that makes extensive use of video in his teaching. No amount of verbal description can take the place of the direct visual feedback video provides. It creates a clarity that is impossible to achieve in any other fashion. Research has shown that almost all sports learning accelerates rapidly with the addition of video. For some students, I find that viewing themselves regularly on video is the most powerful single aspect of the entire visualization training process.

The long-term goal of the visualization training process is to create a stroke that is so solid and consistent that you can execute it virtually indefinitely, first in controlled drill, then in rallies, and finally, under the pressures of competitive play. *Visual Tennis* teaches every player how to do this by helping him develop a system of personal stroke keys.

A stroke key is one aspect of an overall stroke pattern, or more precisely, an image of one aspect of the stroke. By holding the image of the key in the mind's eye while he hits the ball, the player activates the entire stroke pattern. The key provides the player with a mental blueprint to follow in making the swing. Properly developed, the key system gives the player a reliable, automatic method for executing the correct technical stroke pattern.

A stroke key can be any part of the image of the overall stroke. It can be an image of one of the four still frames, or one or more of the checkpoints. On the groundstrokes, for example, I have found that the most effective key is some variation of the image of the finish position. The key can also be a moving image, a kind of mini-movie of the *entire* stroke. In the chapters that follow you will learn how to develop and test various keys, how to determine which keys are effective, or "active," in your game. A final section shows you how to create your own stroke key chart for each stroke. Using stroke keys allows any player to correct even difficult problems in preparation and timing, the kinds of problems that are especially resistant to change in traditional lessons.

Because stroke keys are pictures, they bypass the paralysis and confusion caused by words and verbal commands. The fact is that tennis happens too fast to think about in words. But pure imagery can flow through the mind at the speed your body actually moves on the court. Stroke keys are the perfect medium to guide the complicated interplay between mind and body required to play great tennis.

There is also a related major additional benefit. Developing and using a system of personal stroke keys provide the antidote to the universal sports phenomenon of "choking." Stroke keys can eliminate choking because they give the player a way to keep the mind focused even in very tense situations. Focusing on an active stroke key blocks the entry of distracting thoughts and fears. This intrusion of unwanted internal verbal dialogue is what causes unforced errors on easy balls. Typically, confronted with an open shot, a player tells himself something along the lines of "I *have* to make this shot," or "Good players always make these," etc. Ironically, this kind of expectation creates so much pressure that it almost guarantees the player will make the error he is so desperate to avoid.

The first step in overcoming this fear is often simply admitting it exists. A great many players deny they are afraid, and thus are incapable of addressing the problem. It is important in playing competitively, no matter what the level, to accept the natural fear that goes with pressure, and to give yourself permission to miss easy shots until you become comfortable in the situation. If you are willing to do this, the fear will gradually decrease to a level at which it can be controlled. [1]

In addition to developing your stroke patterns, doing muscle memory corrections, and creating your own system of personal keys, the final aspect of visualization training is doing vis-ualization work *away* from the court. As noted above, research studies have demonstrated the value of this form of mental practice in improving sports performance. In fact, visualization is so powerful that it can produce improved performance even without physical practice. However, the maximum benefit occurs when mental and physical practice are used in combination.

The procedure for doing off-court visualizations is simple: sit down and close your eyes. Some people prefer to do visual work in a quiet, or even a dark environment, others do it to music. Eastern European trainers have their athletes lies down, listen to classical music, and then visualize perfect performances in their individual sports. Whether you lie down or listen to music, the important thing is to be relaxed, comfortable, and motivated. If you have trouble sitting still, it can help to actually get up and swing the racket physically while doing the visualizations.

Starting with one stroke, see yourself execute it perfectly, following the models shown in the individual chapters. Give the image as much detail as possible. Try to see your entire body and your racket. See the brand name on your racket, tennis shoes, tennis clothes, etc. Try visualizing in color if you do not normally do so. Visualize the swing at different speeds. Start in slow motion, and gradually work up to the speed of your swing in actual play. Add the sound of the ball striking the center of the sweet spot. Now shift to the system of personal stroke keys you have devised for the stroke. Focus on each individual key in the context of the overall stroke. Visualize each of your keys. Now repeat the same procedure for each of your other strokes.

As you advance as a player, you can start to visualize shot combinations as well as basic strokes. See yourself hit a forehand, then a backhand, then a forehand, etc. Then put together imaginary points—a serve followed by a winning

---

[1]*This is the point made by Allen Fox in his indispensable book* If I'm the Better Player, Why Can't I Win? *(New York: Simon and Schuster, 1979). It explains how great players accept their fear of choking, and how you can reframe court situations to do this yourself. The book is one of the best analyses ever written of competitive sports psychology, and is probably a prerequisite for certain players in developing their stroke key system.*

first volley, or a return of serve followed by a passing shot. Put together patterns that are typical of the kinds of points you play, or would like to play, in matches. Visualize the combinations that are your strengths, and especially, your weaknesses. (For example, if you have trouble making low first volleys on your forehand, or hitting backhand groundstrokes down the line, see yourself executing a series of these shots.)

Although still outside the mainstream of tennis instructional theory, visualization techniques have recently gained attention as part of the growing interest in sports psychology, and are the subject of a growing number of articles in the tennis press. Typically, these articles advise a player to work on a troublesome shot by "imagining yourself hitting the shot perfectly." The problem with this advice, however, is that it assumes the player knows what a "perfect" shot looks like in the first place. In fact, if the player could see the stroke clearly in his mind's eye, he would probably not need advice on how to improve it through visualization. Worse, by following this advice, he may actually reinforce his technical problems by visualizing flawed technique.

To be truly effective, visualization training must first show the player how to construct a superior technical image of the stroke. Only then can the player benefit from visual practice in any systematic or meaningful way. This is why the majority of this book is dedicated to construction of technical models and stroke keys for each stroke.

A final dimension of a complete visual training program is the use of video images. This means watching video of good stroke technique in order to reinforce your own visual models. Video is also a source of timing, rhythm, and inspiration. Most players have discovered the value of watching great tennis on their own. This same effect should be systematically cultivated. *The Wining Edge* is an example of an instructional video designed to enhance visual modeling, as is *Tennis* with Stan Smith from Sybervision. Taping television matches is a limitless source of additional images.

In addition, I have created a video version of *Visual Tennis*. This video provides clear models for strokes that are unavailable on other instructional videos. These include the straight backswing forehand, the two-handed backhand, the two-handed backhand volley, and the basic serve. Although both the book and the video are designed to be used independently, most students will find it more effective to use them together.

Finally, I recommend that every student make his own personal visual modeling video, if possible. Again, using a home video camera or working with your pro, record a series of perfect practice swings. Do a statueman at the end of each swing to emphasize the checkpoints. Do perfect freeze frames of each aspect of the stroke. Now practice executing the models hitting balls in the controlled drill, preferably against a ball machine.

How much visual practice should the average player do away from the court? This is a question that every player has to answer for himself based on his own experience. Research suggests that the optimum ratio may be as high as an hour of visualization for every three hours spent on the court. If this ratio is correct, it means that it is almost impossible for the average player to do too much visualization.

As a start, try one session of visual practice for every session of actual play. For example, if you play three times a week, have three visualization sessions. Try doing pure visualization in two, and watching video in the other. Start with five to ten minutes of pure visualization, and ten to fifteen minutes of video. If you wish, you can build up the length of your sessions from there. By experimentation, and by working with your pro, find the combinations that keep your interest and enhance the quality and your enjoyment of the game.

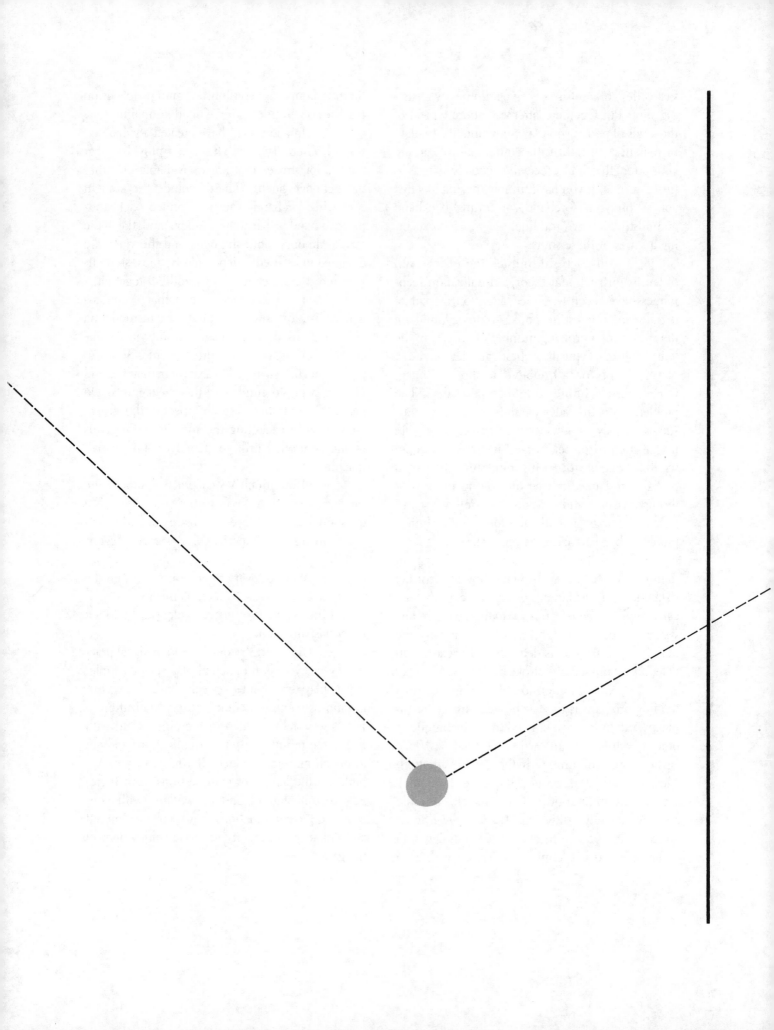

THE CLASSICAL STYLE

Visual Tennis is based on the creation of a series of model strokes. These models could be drawn from any of three predominant styles in the game: the continental style, the western style, or the eastern or classical style. The models I have chosen are of the classical style. This does not mean that the principles of visualization training cannot be applied to either the continental style or the western style. Players who want to play either continental or western tennis could follow the principles outlined in this book simply by creating their own visual models using video and/or still photos of players using those styles.

However, for the majority of players, the classical style will be by far the easiest of the three to develop, and also the most productive in terms of competitive results and aesthetic satisfaction. There are two compelling reasons for this: first, the classical style is *mechanically simpler*, and second, it is more *strategically flexible*.

Compared with continental or western strokes, classical stroke patterns have the fewest number of variables to master, and thus are easier to learn, and also to execute consistently, especially under pressure. The primary technical difference between the three styles is that classical strokes require a minimum use of wrist to execute correctly. This stems from the differences in the forehand grip. With the grip for the continental forehand, part of the palm of the hand is placed *on top* of the racket. At the other extreme, a western forehand grip places part of the palm of the hand *underneath* the racket handle. But the classical forehand grip places almost all of the palm of the hand *behind* the racket, so the palm and the racket head are parallel and naturally aligned.

The grip plays a crucial role in the nature of the forehand stroke because the grip dictates the role of the wrist in the execution of the stroke. Wrist motion is by far the most difficult factor to control in any tennis shot, and is responsible for a majority of technical errors on the forehand. Because of the grip, both the continental and the western forehands require that the wrist be released through the contact with the ball. By releasing the wrist, the player in either of these alternate styles accelerates the racket head upward through the ball, producing topspin.

High-speed photographic studies have shown that whatever style you play, the racket face *must* be vertical at contact to produce spin and ball control. When the wrist is released in the course of the swing, achieving this vertical racket position requires almost perfect timing. Even a slight error in the wrist release can result in the loss of racket head control, and thus, an unforced error. This problem is eliminated in the classical style in which the wrist is not usually released until after impact, if at all.

This is not to say that literally every tennis player should follow the classical style. There are certain advantages to the continental and the western games. Continental strokes are based on taking the ball on the rise. By hitting the ball on the rise, players generate additional pace from the speed of the ball as it accelerates upward off the court. At the same time, by taking the ball earlier, they cut down the time the opponent has to recover from his shot, and react to the next ball. Continental tennis is well suited to fast court surfaces, most notably grass, and to playing the serve and volley game.

At the other end of the spectrum, the western style is often superior on slower surfaces, especially clay. The western style relies on large looping swing patterns that produce exaggerated topspin. Generally, western-style players allow the ball to drop slightly below the top of the bounce before making contact. This allows them the extra time necessary for making the exaggerated western swings. If he has truly mastered this heavy topspin style, the western player is very difficult to outrally, and his groundstrokes are superior to hitting passing shots because of the dipping action caused by the additional topspin.

Despite the undeniable successes recorded by players in both these technical traditions, the difficulties of the western and continental styles are prohibitive for the majority of recreational, and even tournament players. Because of the central role of the wrist release, playing continental or western tennis well requires vastly superior hand-eye coordination. It also requires significantly more practice to develop and maintain. Few players have the phenomenal timing that allows John McEnroe to hit every ball on the rise. Fewer still have the time and determination of a Bjorn Borg, who spent four hours a day hitting against a wall to perfect his forehand wrist roll. Compared with these styles, the classical style can be learned much more quickly by players regardless of natural ability and available practice time.

An additional advantage is that with classical strokes it is possible to hit the ball equally well on the rise, at the top of the bounce, or, slightly on the way down. Classical players can take the ball early on every shot as do Jimmy Connors and Andre Agassi. They can play it just after the top of the bounce the way Chris Evert does. Or they can vary their timing to the court and the opponent following the style of Ivan Lendl, who takes the ball early in some matches, and lets it drop slightly in others. Most recreational and even tournament players will naturally tend to hit the ball as it drops, but there are exceptions at all levels of the game. With classical strokes, every player can experiment with the timing of the strokes for himself.

In addition to its technical simplicity, the second major advantage of the classical style is its strategic flexibility. Most players lack the ability to play winning serve and volley tennis against every opponent. Conversely, baseliners have difficulty winning points quickly on faster courts, especially against weaker players. Most players maximize their success by playing a combination of attacking and backcourt tennis. Against some opponents, they should take the net at every opportunity. Other opponents should be played primarily from the backcourt. Most matches, however, require you to mix these two styles depending on the situation. The goal is to use your relative strengths against the relative weaknesses of each opponent. Thus, your strategy should be chosen for its effectiveness against a given opponent, on a given court, on a given day. This mix of attacking and baseline strategies is called the all-court game.

Compared with continental or western tennis, the classical style is much better suited to playing the all-court game. It is possible to attack or to defend in any combination, and with equal success, if you play classical tennis. This is particularly true on hard court surfaces, which have become the standard in the United States, and, increasingly, around the world.

It is this dual advantage of strategic flexibility and technical simplicity that makes the classical style the best choice for the majority of players at all levels. This conclusion does not imply that classical players cannot learn from players using a different style. All players should try to imitate the fabulous shoulder turns on the groundstrokes of a McEnroe or a Borg. Despite his continental groundstrokes, McEnroe's volleys are perfect technical models for classical players. The same could be said of the service motion of many western-style players, including Borg. However, classical strokes offer a simpler and more effective overall approach to playing your best tennis.

How do classical-style players stand in comparison with champions of the two other styles, and what players can we draw on to create the models for classical strokes? It is fair to say that over time, and particularly in the modern era, classical tennis has been the dominant style, with more great champions to serve as technical models than the other two styles combined.

The origins of the classical style in tennis go back to Bill Tilden, who dethroned the western-style champion Bill Johnston as the world's top player in the 1920s. Tilden dominated the game in his era more completely than any player since, winning the U.S. title seven times

and Wimbledon three times, the last Wimbledon title coming in 1930 when Tilden was thirty-seven. Tilden was immediately followed by a second dominant classical champion, Ellsworth Vines, a powerful all-court player, also a winner at Wimbledon and twice U.S. champion in 1931 and 1932. Then came Don Budge, a flawless stylist, and the player who defined the Grand Slam of tennis by winning Wimbledon, the French, the American, and the Australian titles in a single year for the first time in 1938. The next great classical champion was Jack Kramer, the dominant force in tennis in the 1940s, who also established the serve and volley strategy as a permanent aspect of the modern game.

Ken Rosewall, Tony Trabert, and John Newcombe are among the other outstanding classical players who have found their places in tennis history. Rosewall, who won five major singles titles, possessed a backhand that was the virtual archetype of the one-handed underspin drive. Trabert, who had an extremely solid all-around classical game, hit the ball with more depth and topspin than other players of his era, and in 1955, won three of the four Grand Slam legs, missing only the Australian title. Newcombe, who won the U.S. title twice and Wimbledon three times, used classical strokes to play an extremely aggressive serve and volley game. His forehand, with its loop backswing, minimal use of wrist, and smooth high finish, still remains one of the best models for that variation of the stroke.

In the history of the women's game, the dominance of the classical style is even more pronounced. Alice Marble, Helen Wills Moody, Maureen Connolly, Margaret Court, and Billie Jean King are all outstanding examples of players with classical stroke patterns. They also are the greatest players in the women's game before the Open era. Only Suzanne Lenglen, the athletic French champion of the 1920s played with a different technical style, the continental. There has yet to be a great women's champion with western strokes.

The classical women's champions use

a mixture of strategies, as did their male counterparts. Thus, Alice Marble, who played the serve and volley in the 1930s, as well as Margaret Court and Billie Jean King all adapted classical technique to an attacking style. Maureen Connolly, and Helen Wills Moody, on the other hand, achieved equal success playing classical tennis from the baseline.

With the beginning of modern professional tennis, the definition of who is a classical player becomes more complex for several reasons, including the introduction of the two-handed backhand as a dominant stroke, the advent of heavy or exaggerated topspin, and the dramatically increased shot velocity with the evolution of racket technology. Yet the majority of the great players in the 1970s and 1980s can still be clearly identified by their classical technical strokes. The list includes top men players such as Stan Smith, Vitas Gerulaitis, Sandy Mayer, and Brian Gottfried. Among the women, examples are Virginia Wade, Hana Mandlikova, and Tracy Austin.

The list also includes four players who have dominated the game in the 1980s: Chris Evert, Jimmy Connors, Martina Navratilova, and Ivan Lendl. Most recently we can add Steffi Graf, Michael Chang, and Andre Agassi to the list of great classical players.

In some respects, the games of these modern classical players could not appear to be more varied. Chris Evert is the prototype of the ultra-steady, two-handed baseliner. Martina Navratilova is one of the great pure serve and volley players. Jimmy Connors hits the ball early and almost completely flat. His game is based on natural aggressiveness and incredible shot making. Ivan Lendl is known for his power, topspin, and consistency, a combination that allows him to win on a variety of court surfaces. Steffi Graf plays primarily from the baseline with a one-handed backhand, but hits the ball harder than any other woman currently in the game. Agassi is every bit as aggressive as Connors, but hits the ball with more topspin, and possibly, with even more pace.

What is not usually recognized is that all these champions have basic technical similarities that place them within the bounds of the classical tradition. Their variations in strategy of play only demonstrate the supreme versatility of classical stroke production. The way these players strike the ball gives them more in common with one another than with other players who may play a similar strategic style. As we have just seen, classical tennis is not defined by strategy. It is equally well suited to the baseline or the attacking game. Neither is it defined by the nature and amount of spin a player uses. A player may hit various shots with topspin, with underspin, or hit them flat, and still play classical tennis. Playing within the classical style it is possible to hit the ball as flat as Connors, with a moderate degree of topspin as Evert, Navratilova, Agassi, and Graf do, or with heavier topspin as does Lendl. Further, it is possible to play classical tennis with either the one-handed or two-handed backhand.

Rather than strategy or spin, the classical style can best be defined in terms of more basic factors of grip and bio-mechanics of stroke production. At base, the strokes of all great classical players share five elements in common:

1. Some version of an eastern forehand grip. This is combined with an eastern or continental backhand grip for the one-handed backhand, or a left-handed forehand grip for the two-handed backhand.

2. The use of compact swing patterns with a minimum of wrist and with the hitting arm close to the body.

3. Vertical swing planes, with the racket perpendicular to the court, and smooth, high follow-throughs.

4. The use of the legs and of body rotation—body leverage—to generate maximum power and spin.

5. A feeling of effortlessness, fluidity, and rhythm that makes classical tennis look, and feel, easy.

All of the players mentioned above use variations of the eastern forehand grip. Evert and Navratilova are close to having "pure" eastern grips, while Connors, Graf, Agassi, and Lendl all have various versions of the "modified" eastern grip that rotates the palm position slightly downward toward the underside of the racket. None of these players rotate the palm far enough, however, to reach the extreme position of the western grip, where the palm is turned under the racket handle. All have the bulk of their palms squarely positioned behind the racket handle, and this position is the basis for a classical forehand stroke.

The second component of the classical forehand is the use of a compact swing pattern, which eliminates, or minimizes, the role of the wrist. The role of the wrist in stroke production is one of the most widely misunderstood aspects of the game, and the subject of contradictory advice. A common tennis tip advises every player to "keep a firm wrist" on the forehand. But an equally popular school of thought argues that the wrist should be released at contact to generate additional racket head speed.

As the photos in the forehand chapter demonstrate, both these views are an inaccurate description of the wrist position on a good classical forehand. One of the distinguishing characteristics of the forehand swing of classical players is not a stiff or "firm" wrist. Rather, the wrist is slightly laid back at contact with the ball. Keeping a firm wrist implies that the wrist and arm should stay straight in line on the forehand. This will cause the hit to be late, make the swing stiff, and dramatically reduce both power and spin. On the other hand, releasing the wrist through the contact will lead to a loss of racket head control, reduced body leverage, and thus a loss in shot velocity.

In the forehand turn position for each of the players identified above, the elbow is slightly tucked in toward the waist, and the wrist is at an angle to the forearm, laid back so that the racket points vertically at the rear fence of the court. This arm position is called the double bend position. The arm stays in this double bend position— elbow in, wrist back—at the contact point, all the way through to the finish position. This arm position creates what is known as a "compact" swing pattern. In the compact swing, the arm and body move together in unison. The arm stays in, and this eliminates the common error of using too large a swing. The double bend position keeps the classical player from using too much backswing and/ or a rolled, uncontrolled followthrough.

If the wrist releases at all in the classical swing, it is as a relaxation response, and this occurs after the contact with the ball. The fact is that it is impossible to make early contact with the ball on a classical forehand unless the wrist is at least somewhat laid back. For the sake of simplicity, the models presented here demonstrate the wrist staying in this position throughout the stroke. The vast majority of players, I have found, only invite inconsistency and loss of power with any variety of wrist movement in their basic stroke pattern. In the classical forehand, the wrist is released at contact only as a last resort, for example, when running wide and stretching to get the racket on the ball, or to hit topspin when the ball is short or very low. Commentators who state that Ivan Lendl has a "wristy" forehand have never closely examined still frames of his stroke pattern. What often misleads observers is Lendl's closed face backswing. As we shall see in the chapter on the forehand, this is actually a technical advance in the nature of the backswing. It allows Lendl to maintain the essential elements of the classical forehand while hitting with as much or more velocity than any player in the game.

The third factor going into a classical stroke is the nature of the swing plane. Unlike the continental and western forehands, where the face of the racket turns over during the course of the swing, the classical forehand is based on a *vertical swing path*. This means that the racket head stays vertical, or *perpendicular*, to the court surface from ready position all the way through to the finish. Even if the wrist relaxes on the followthrough, it never turns the racket face over in relation to the plane of the court.

Topspin is a natural aspect of the classical stroke because the racket face starts below the contact point with the ball, and is accelerating upward at contact. This upward acceleration causes the racket face to brush upward across the back side of the ball, and the ball to rotate over itself, that is, to rotate with topspin, as it travels back toward the opponent. With a vertical swing path, the classical player can produce natural topspin. This means that topspin results automatically from the proper execution of the stroke without extra or conscious effort. This contrasts with the continental or western forehand (as well as an improperly hit eastern forehand) where topspin is generated by releasing the wrist at contact to increase racket head acceleration.

Another advantage of the classical style is that it not only allows a player to produce natural topspin, it allows him to vary the amount of topspin without changing his basic stroke. By accelerating the racket upward more sharply at contact, the player increases the brushing effect on the back of the ball, and this creates additional spin. Conversely, by moving the racket head through the ball on a slightly straighter line, the player can decrease the amount of spin, hitting the ball with a flatter trajectory.

A crucial aspect in generating this natural topspin is a high, complete followthrough. A logical question asked by students is: why worry about the followthrough when the ball is already off the strings? The answer is that the followthrough determines how the racket is moving at the contact, and is a crucial factor in the nature of the stroke. As discussed in detail in the individual stroke chapters, a full, high followthrough means that the racket will be accelerating at the contact point, and this acceleration is what produces pace as well as topspin.

The fourth factor that defines the classical style is the role of body leverage, the shoulders and the legs, in producing the stroke. The legendary tennis instructor Tom Stow, who coached Don Budge when he won the first Grand Slam, was once asked to reduce tennis to three words. His reply was: "Turn your shoulders." Allowed three more words, he might have added: "Coil your legs." The shoulders and the legs, rather than an exaggerated swing, are the key to maximizing power in classical tennis. Thus, in the preparation for the stroke, the position of the body at the turn is critical. As we will see in the sequence photos that follow, the shoulders must be turned fully sideways so that they are perpendicular to the net. Next, as the player steps into the shot, the knees should be fully coiled just prior to the start of the foreswing. If the shoulders are turned and the knees coiled before the racket starts forward, the classical player will automatically produce great body leverage. The rotation of the shoulders and the uncoiling of the legs will generate increased acceleration of the racket head as it moves toward the ball. This will be translated into shot velocity and topspin.

This brings us to the fifth and final characteristic of classical players—their relaxed, fluid appearance. They make playing great tennis look effortless. The reason for this is rooted in the nature of the classical style. Classical players appear to be working less hard because they minimize mechanical variables and maximize body leverage. Classical players generate effortless power, and play with an understated ease. Classical strokes are simply more efficient—there is less to do to hit the ball correctly. If you master classical stroke patterns, your game will take on this appearance, and it will have a corresponding feel. You cannot really understand the physical and aesthetic pleasure of playing this kind of tennis until you have played it yourself.

In the following chapters this is what you will learn how to do. Each chapter sets out a model for the particular stroke. In some cases, there is a basic model, and then one or more variations. On the forehand, for example, the basic forehand model uses a straight backswing, but the circular backswing and the closed face backswing developed by Ivan Lendl are presented as variations. On the backhand, there are models for the one-handed topspin backhand, the one-handed slice backhand variation, and the two-handed backhand. Furthermore, each chapter discusses how to decide which particular model, or models, to incorporate into your own game.

What I have done in the individual chapters is to try to strip away the personal variations each player develops and reduce the stroke patterns to the fewest number of possible elements. This approach provides the cleanest possible models for each stroke, models that each player can absorb and synthesize into a stroke pattern marked with his own personality and flair. If you observe players trained in the visualization system, you will see that their strokes share the basic technical elements presented here, and are usually highly reliable and effective, but no two look exactly the same. There are going to be differences in the exact length and shape of the swing, and in the amount of body rotation, spin, pace, leg action, etc., but these all are differences that fall within the boundaries of the classical tradition.

The reality is that no player will ever execute the model stroke with absolute perfection on a regular basis. The model stroke serves only as an ideal that students should strive to approximate. Its great value is in giving every player a precise image of what he is trying to do. On the court, a player who can execute his stroke models with 80 to 90 percent accuracy will consistently excellent tennis, and, over time, develop his full potential for the game.

Despite the stroke variations and the flexibility of the models presented here, it is more than possible that other players and teaching pros will have different definitions of the "correct" classical stroke patterns. For example, some pros may disagree with my view on the acceptable range of forehand grips, or they may advocate a more extreme grip on the one-handed backhand. Others might advocate a larger, less compact backswing on the basic forehand model, or argue that the backhand backswing should be taught from the beginning with an upward looping motion. They may disagree with my belief in the necessity of a high service toss, or the footwork I advocate on the advanced serve. They may reject my emphasis on the role of shoulder rotation in the volley. Others may feel my stroke models place too much emphasis on the length and precision of the followthrough, or they may disagree with my view on an absolute minimum use of wrist.

This list undoubtedly does not exhaust the points of potential critical disagreement. In my opinion, however, none of these objections should distract from the fundamental question posed by this book—the issue of how best to teach the game. I believe that the models I have chosen provide the simplest choices for teaching sound technical strokes, and doing it in the shortest possible time. I also believe that the superiority of the models I have chosen can be easily demonstrated by working with students on the teaching court, and I encourage other teachers to prove this to themselves. But to those who choose to define classical stroke patterns differently, I say that visualization teaching technology provides the best possible chance for actually putting them into practice, as it is the only approach that works with the body's natural learning process.

The fact is that the majority of players already use some version of the classical grips, and the majority of teaching pros profess to teach some version of classical stroke patterns. The problem most players face is not in choosing how they hold the racket, or how they would like to hit the ball, but in translating those choices into effective, consistent strokes. If you go to most tennis clubs, it is common to see players gripping the racket correctly, but stroking the ball quite poorly, due to inconsistent swing patterns, inadequate shoulder turns, uncontrolled wrist action, late contact, poor leg work, or some combination of all of the above.

The failure of most players to play better lies not so much in the players themselves, or in the efforts of their instructors, but rather, in the nature of tennis instruction itself. Visualization training overcomes this fundamental weakness by approaching the game in the same way that great players have always done—instinctively, naturally, visually.

THE FOREHAND

The forehand is the most basic shot in tennis, and the stroke most players learn first. Typically, it becomes at least somewhat consistent fairly quickly, and develops into their best shot. At higher levels of play, however, this tendency is frequently reversed. Top players are often more inconsistent on the forehand side. A well-known television commentator once remarked that there were only four players in the world with good forehands. A similar pattern can also occur in recreational tennis and sectional tournament play. As a player improves and faces better competition, his forehand becomes less reliable than his backhand. How can this phenomenon be explained? More importantly, how can a player build a reliable forehand that will hold up no matter how advanced his level of play may become?

The answers to these questions lie in the technical nature of the stroke. While there is no doubt that a forehand is an easier motion for most players to learn, in some respects it is actually a more technically complex shot than the backhand, due to the position of the shoulders. To make a correct swing on the forehand, it is necessary first to turn the shoulders perpendicular to the net, and then, to rotate them back a full ninety degrees, to parallel with the net. This rotation, while relatively easy with low paced balls hit by beginning and intermediate players, becomes more and more difficult to achieve as the velocity of the rallies increases at higher levels of play. There is a common tendency for players at higher levels to abandon correct coordination of the body rotation and to rely more and more on the arm and wrist to execute the shot. This leads to inconsistency on the forehand side. This is also frequently true with recreational players who learn to get the ball over the net using the arm and wrist.

As they improve, and face better players, they are unable to execute the stroke consistently and make numerous unforced errors when they try to rely on wrist action to generate velocity and hit forcing shots.

Most of the truly great players have developed forehands that maximize the use of body leverage and minimize the role of the arm and wrist—players such as Ivan Lendl, Andre Agassi, Steffi Graf, and Chris Evert. Even the players who play with a western or continental style, Bjorn Borg, Boris Becker, or John McEnroe, have forehands that are built on superior shoulder rotation, and use of the legs for power. In this chapter you will learn a stroke model which relies on body leverage and a minimum of arm and wrist motion to execute. If you use the principles of visualization to master the forehand bio-mechanics, you will build a stroke that will be consistent and powerful at any level of play.

The classical forehand stroke demonstrated here can be hit well with either of two variations on the same basic eastern grip, as demonstrated in the grip chapter. I call these the classic eastern and the modified eastern. Both grips place the bulk of the palm of the hand directly *behind* the racket handle. Players such as Chris Evert and Martina Navratilova are close to the pure eastern grip, with Martina's grip verging on a mild continental. Lendl, Agassi, Graf, and Jimmy Connors, on the other hand, have modified eastern grips, which are rotated slightly downward toward the western.

Is there a relationship between the variations in the classical grip and the spin the player produces? Both Evert and Navratilova hit with moderate topspin, while Lendl and Agassi have heavier ball rotation. This would suggest that to achieve more spin, a player should shift toward the modified eastern. Connors, however, also uses the modified eastern grip, and he hits the ball almost completely flat. While it is true that grip plays a role in the degree of spin, it is only one factor. More important is the actual swing path the racket takes. Topspin comes from the rapid

upward acceleration of the racket face at ball contact. Thus, the correct, low racket position at the start of the foreswing is crucial to generate ball rotation. Unless the player masters a consistent stroke pattern incorporating this, he will never hit topspin consistently, no matter which grip he uses.

The primary factor, then, in deciding on your own forehand grip is not spin, but rather what feels comfortable, and what produces consistent results. If you are unsure, begin by trying the classical, or pure eastern grip. Then slide your grip slightly downward to the modified eastern position, and experiment with it. Most players, I find, tend to be more comfortable with this modified version. In terms of the stroke pattern, either can be the basis of a correct technical stroke, so it is up to you, in conjunction with your teaching pro, to find the variation you prefer.

The other major variable in the classical forehand swing pattern is the backswing. Should you learn the stroke with a simple, straight backswing, or with a circular loop, as is commonly taught by teaching pros? From the purely theoretical point of view, it could be argued that the loop is superior. This is because, with the loop, the racket head is in continuous motion. It travels in a circular path, and thus, there is unbroken acceleration toward ball contact. With the straight backswing, there is a slight pause, because, when the racket goes straight back, it must then stop, shift directions, and then start forward to the ball. Theoretically, then, the loop should generate slightly more racket head speed, and also be more fluid and rhythmic.

In my experience, however, the "theoretical" advantage of the loop rarely results in better forehands. The reverse is usually the case. Players who are taught the loop seem always to exaggerate the motion. Typically, the circular backswing becomes too large and too time consuming. The player often ends up with a gigantic swing, flailing at the ball with his arm and wrist, generating only a fraction of his potential power, and making far more than his share of unforced errors. Remember that a fundamental aspect of classical tennis is the use of *body leverage* to produce ball velocity. As we will see when we turn to the model stroke, this means that the arm must stay in the double bend position, and remain fairly close to the body throughout the stroke. This allows the shoulders and legs to play a central role in the stroke. The circular backswing tends to reduce or eliminate these crucial elements. With a large, circular swing, the arm and racket tend to move independently, instead of in smooth coordination with the rest of the body.

The straight backswing preserves the coordination of all the stroke elements in the forehand. It is also far simpler to learn. The most crucial aspect of the backswing is the position of the racket head at the moment it starts forward to the ball. With the straight motion, the racket head goes directly to the correct position, low and close to the body. Beginners feel the strength of this racket position almost immediately. Players who learn the loop often never master this correct arm and racket position, and are unable to hit up on the ball to develop topspin.

For these reasons, the primary model in this chapter is the straight backswing. If you closely observe players such as Evert and Connors, two good examples of this variety of the stroke, you will notice something interesting: although the backswing is beautifully compact, the racket head never actually stops moving. There is a small elliptical loop as the racket changes direction from backward to forward. By focusing on a straight backswing, most players will naturally develop this minimal looping motion, which preserves racket head speed and aids rhythm and timing. Stressing the full circular loop, on the other hand, will destroy other important basic elements in the stroke, and create problems that are difficult to correct later.

Having said this, I am also presenting two other versions of the backswing as *variations*. The first is the larger, classical loop discussed above. This is shown for two reasons. First, a certain percentage of players will naturally, on their own, progress from the straight backswing to the loop. If the basic mechanics of the stroke are sound, this will not cause problems, and in fact, may add slightly greater racket head speed. If this motion is natural, and producing solid stroke production, it would be counterproductive to force an arbitrary change to the straight backswing. Also, players who have learned the loop originally, but are now struggling with the stroke, sometimes do better by correcting a faulty loop, rather than trying to change to the straight backswing.

The second backswing variation presented here is the closed face loop. This is the backswing developed by Ivan Lendl. His forehand will go down as one of the best in the history of tennis. It is a model of technical excellence, power, consistency, and ball control. Yet many players, teaching pros, and commentators think of it as an unorthodox, and even idiosyncratic shot. However, I believe Lendl's forehand represents an advance in the evolution of the classical style.

The closed face backswing has mesmerized and confused most observers so that they fail to note the crucial elements the stroke shares in common with other classical forehands. These include the tremendous application of body leverage through shoulder rotation and the uncoiling of the legs, and also the double bend position of the hitting arm. A common criticism of Lendl's stroke pattern is that it is "wristy." However, still frame analysis clearly shows that he makes contact with the wrist laid back, and the elbow tucked in toward the waist—the double bend arm position associated with the classical forehand swing pattern. The wrist release, if any, comes after the ball is off the strings, and is a relaxation response at the end of the followthrough, rather than a part of the actual bio-mechanics of the stroke. As outlined in the introduction, one characteristic of any classical stroke pattern is a vertical swing plane. Lendl's closed face backswing preserves this element as well. While it is true that the face is closed through the course of the backswing, it quickly becomes vertical as it approaches contact, a position that is maintained in the course of the followthrough.

This closed face backswing is a technical advance in three respects. First, it eliminates the major danger of the open face loop, the tendency for the arm to move independently, and thus, reduce the use of body leverage in the stroke. With the face closed, the elbow is literally forced in toward the body at the completion of the backswing, so that the arm is in the correct position and the shot can be generated with the hitting arm, shoulders, and legs working in unison. Second, by closing the face, Lendl makes the circular backswing motion much more compact than with the larger traditional loop. The racket still travels in a circular path, picking up additional racket head speed, but since the circle is smaller, the path is much shorter. This allows Lendl to execute the entire stroke more rapidly, an advantage given the extremely high ball velocity of modern pro tennis.

With the large loop, some players, even at the recreational level, are unable to get the racket around to contact in time, causing their forehands to break down against powerful opponents. With the closed face backswing, the player can generate as much or more racket head speed as with the large loop, but do so in less time, ensuring early contact.

The third advantage to the closed face loop is the production of greater topspin. As the sequence photos of this backswing show, the position of the racket at the completion of the backswing is *lower* than either the straight backswing, or the traditional loop. This means that as the racket starts forward to the contact, the angle of the swing plane is steeper. Since the racket is moving upward more sharply at the contact point, the brushing effect on the backside of the ball is greater, and thus, the stroke will have increased topspin. Using the closed face backswing Lendl has maximized the amount of topspin that can be generated within the technical boundaries of the classical style.

This conclusion does not imply, however, that all or even most recreational players should adopt the closed face loop. As noted, for a beginner, the straight backswing is by far the easiest to master. It simply has the fewest variables, and is likely to lead to solid forehand stroke production in the shortest period of time. However, for advanced players, or for players who are struggling with a traditional loop backswing, the closed face is a potential option. If you are late at contact with your looped forehand or, if your stroke lacks power, experiment with the closed face. Properly executed, it will maximize your body leverage, as well as produce greater consistency.

Whichever backswing you develop, your forehand should preserve the crucial technical elements of classical stroke production. The classical forehand allows you to hit a stroke with superior pace and consistency, with the minimum number of technical variables. This will allow you to maintain a high level of execution as you improve and advance to higher and higher levels of recreational or competitive play. The following teaching progressions will show you how to do this for yourself.

CREATING THE FOREHAND SWING PATTERN

In the following sections, you will learn to hit the forehand using the principles of visualization training. Through a combination of special sequence photos and text, you will create a precise *physical* and *visual* model. This model will become your personal blueprint for developing the stroke.

First, the forehand is presented from the front view and broken down into its component parts. Accompanying this sequence is a description of the genereal technical characteristics of the stroke. Then the stroke is shown simultaneously from both the front and the side views. In these two sequences, the four key still frames are identified. These still frames will become the building blocks for learning the model stroke. They are:

1. **The Ready Position**
2. **The Turn**
3. **The Contact Point**
4. **The Finish Position**

If you observe the still frames in the context of the overall stroke pattern, you will see that passing through each of the still frames correctly will guarantee that the entire swing pattern is correct as well. In simple terms, if the swing is correct at the Ready Position, at the Turn, at the Contact Point, and at the Finish Position, it will *have* to be correct at every point in between as well.

In the following section, you will then learn how to master each of the four still frames individually, through a series of detailed checkpoints. Then you will put the correct still frames together into a complete forehand swing pattern. After, you will learn how to do muscle memory corrections, allowing you to correct your mistakes as they occur in the learning process. Finally, you will learn to create your own personal system of stroke keys for the forehand that will allow you to hit the stroke consistently in rallies and in match play.

The basic learning progressions are demonstrated with the straight backswing, which, as discussed in the introduction to this chapter, is the simplest, most reliable, and easiest to learn. In addition, however, the two backswing variations discussed above are included: the circular backswing, and the closed face circular backswing. There are also stroke keys for both variations.

1	2	3	4	5
READY POSITION	**START OF TURN**	**THE TURN**	**STEP TO BALL**	**START OF SWING**

Characteristics of the Forehand
FRONT VIEW

○ ○

Grip: The forehand begins with an eastern grip which places as much of the palm of the hand as possible directly *behind* the face of the racket. This can be seen in Frame 2, above, and also in Frame 6, where the hand is squarely supporting the racket face at contact. The proper grip ensures that the stroke will be hit with the minimum number of variables, and this simplicity is the key to consistent execution. If you are unsure about how to achieve the correct grip, the two major classical variations are demonstrated in the grip chapter.

Minimum Use of Wrist: The forehand is executed with virtually no wrist movement throughout the course of the stroke. Instead, the arm and wrist are already in the double bend position in the Ready Position (Frame 1), with the wrist slightly laid back and the elbow tucked in toward the waist. This position is maintained at the Turn (Frame 3), at the Contact Point (Frame 6), all the way through to the Finish Position (Frame 9). This distinguishes the classical forehand from both the western

32

6
CONTACT POINT

7
START OF FOLLOWTHROUGH

8
FOLLOWTHROUGH

9
FINISH POSITION

and the continental, which rely on the release of the wrist at impact. If the wrist releases at all in the classical stroke, it is as a relaxation response that begins near or after the Finish Position shown above. For the purposes of the model, the correct laid back position is shown here throughout the course of the stroke.

Vertical Swing Path: In the classical forehand swing pattern, the racket face remains *vertical*, or perpendicular, to the court surface throughout the course of the motion. In the Ready Position (Frame 1), the racket starts in the correct vertical position. This is maintained as the motion starts (Frame 2). At the completion of the Turn (Frame 3), the racket face is still straight up and down. This position is maintained throughout the course of the forward swing as well, at the Contact Point (Frame 6), all the way to the Finish Position (Frame 9).

Natural Topspin and Power: With a vertical swing plane the forehand stroke will produce natural topspin and shot velocity. These are generated by the swing path, the rotation of the shoulders, and the uncoiling of the legs. In the Ready Position (Frame 1), the shoulders start parallel to the net. At the Turn (Frame 3), they have rotated ninety degrees and are perpendicular. At the Contact Point (Frame 6) they are rotating back into the ball, until they are again parallel to the net at the Finish Position (Frame 9). In the Ready Position (Frame 1), the knees are flexed. At the Step to Ball (Frame 4), they are fully coiled. At the Contact Point (Frame 6), the knees uncoil into the shot, remaining slightly flexed in the Finish Position (Frame 9). This body rotation, combined with the uncoiling of the legs, causes the racket face to accelerate sharply, brushing up the backside of the ball at contact, generating power and spin.

Forehand: Four Key Still Frames
SIDE VIEW

○○○○○○○○○○○○○○○○○○○○○○○○○○○○○○○○○○○○

STILL FRAME #1　　　　　　　　　　　**STILL FRAME #2**

READY POSITION　　　**START OF TURN**　　　**THE TURN**　　　**STEP TO BALL**

Forehand: Four Key Still Frames
FRONT VIEW

○○○○○○○○○○○○○○○○○○○○○○○○○○○○○○○○○

STILL FRAME #1　　　　　　　　　　　**STILL FRAME #2**

READY POSITION　　　**START OF TURN**　　　**THE TURN**　　　**STEP TO BALL**

34

STILL FRAME #4

STILL FRAME #3

START OF SWING CONTACT POINT FOLLOWTHROUGH FINISH POSITION

STILL FRAME #4

STILL FRAME #3

   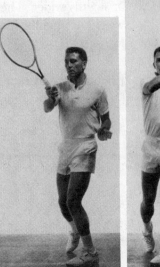

START OF SWING CONTACT POINT FOLLOWTHROUGH FINISH POSITION

Still Frame 1
The Ready Position

○ ○ ○ ○ ○ ○ ○ ○ ○ ○ ○ ○ ○ ○ ○

Checkpoints:

1. *The Shoulders:* The shoulders are parallel to the net in the Ready Position. The upper body is straight up and down from the waist. The bend is in the knees, not at the waist.

2. *The Hitting Arm:* The hitting arm is already in the double bend position. This means that the elbow is tucked in toward the waist, and the wrist is slightly laid back.

3. *The Racket:* The racket is slightly below waist level. It points directly at the net, and the face of the racket is perpendicular to the court surface.

4. *The Legs:* The legs are shoulder width apart, or slightly wider. The knees are flexed, and the weight is slightly forward on the balls of the feet.

Establish the Ready Position physically using the checkpoints, then create the visual image.

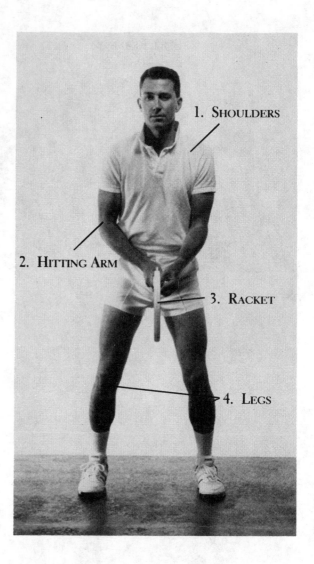

Still Frame 2
The Turn Position

○ ○ ○ ○ ○ ○ ○ ○ ○ ○ ○ ○ ○ ○

Checkpoints:

1. *The Shoulders:* The shoulders have rotated ninety degrees, moving from parallel to perpendicular to the net. The left shoulder is pointing directly at the net. The head is turned slightly to follow the oncoming ball.

2. *The Hitting Arm:* The hitting arm has rotated with the shoulders and remains in the double bend position. The elbow is tucked in toward the waist, and the wrist is laid back. This arm position naturally places the racket slightly below waist level.

3. *The Racket:* The racket has traveled straight back along a line, until the head points directly at the back fence. The *shaft* of the racket is parallel to the court. The butt of the racket is visible to the opponent. The *face* of the racket is still perpendicular to the court.

4. *The Legs:* Both feet have pivoted sideways and are pointing to the side fence. The weight is on the right pivot foot, and the left toes are used for balance. The knees are still flexed.

Move from the Ready Position to the Turn and establish the position physically using the checkpoints, then create the visual image.

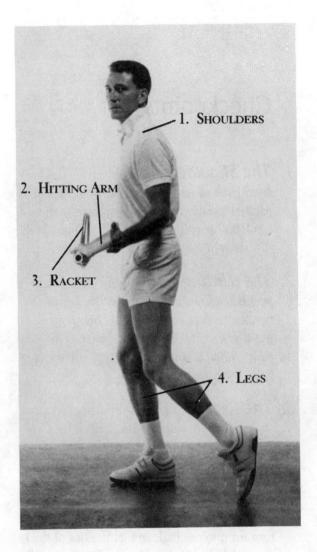

1. SHOULDERS

2. HITTING ARM

3. RACKET

4. LEGS

Still Frame 3
The Contact Point

○ ○ ○ ○ ○ ○ ○ ○ ○ ○ ○ ○ ○ ○

Checkpoints:

1. The Shoulders: The right shoulder has ⸱
tated back roughly halfway toward the origiⁱ
parallel position, and is positioned solidly ᵇ
hind the arm and racket. The upper body
still straight up and down at the waist.

2. The Hitting Arm: The hitting arm ᵇ
pushed the racket forward to the contact. T
double bend position remains unchanged, w
the elbow in and the wrist laid back. This creaᵗ
early contact, and ensures the full transfer
body leverage into the ball.

3. The Racket: The racket has moved forwₐ
and slightly upward to the ball. The Cont
Point is early, well in front of the front leg. T
shaft of the racket is still parallel, and the *fₐ*
perpendicular to the court surface.

4. The Legs: The left front foot has stepₚ
forward into the ball, so that the tips of the tᵉ
are parallel along the edge of a straight liⁱ
The weight is transferred forward to the left fᵉ
and the knees are still bent, but have uncoⁱ
slightly into the ball.

Move from the Ready Position to the Turn, ₐ
forward to the Contact Point. Establish the ₚ ⁻
sition physically using the checkpoints, then
create the visual image.

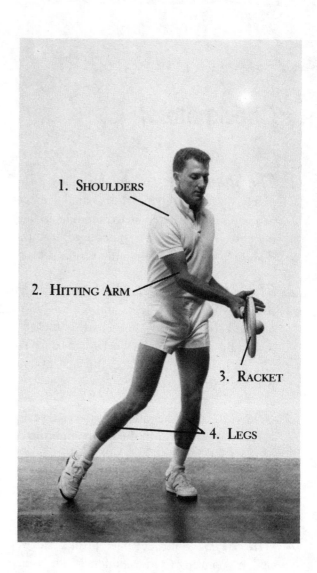

1. SHOULDERS

2. HITTING ARM

3. RACKET

4. LEGS

Still Frame 4
The Finish Position

○ ○ ○ ○ ○ ○ ○ ○ ○ ○ ○ ○ ○ ○ ○

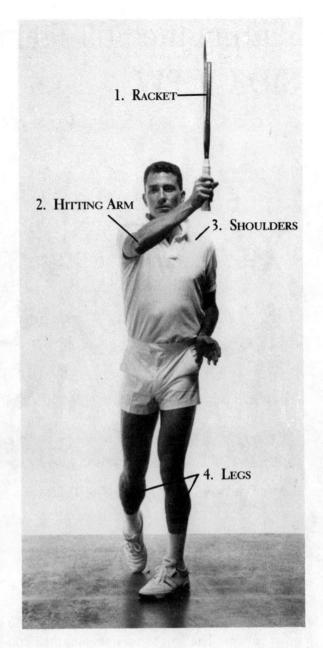

1. RACKET

2. HITTING ARM

3. SHOULDERS

4. LEGS

Checkpoints:

1. The Racket: The racket has accelerated all the way to the Finish Position. The wrist is at eye level. The shaft of the racket is straight up and down with the butt of the racket pointing down at the court. The face of the racket is perpendicular to the left shoulder and to the net.

2. The Hitting Arm: At the finish, the hitting arm is still in the double bend position, with the elbow about thirty degrees from parallel to the court. The wrist remains slightly laid back, and has not released at impact, or through the course of the followthrough.

3. The Shoulders: The shoulders have rotated a full ninety degrees until they are once again parallel to the net. The upper body is still straight up and down from the waist.

4. The Legs: The weight is now fully forward on the left front foot, and the right toes are used for balance. The knees have uncoiled into the ball, but remain slightly flexed.

Move from the Ready Position to the Turn, the Contact, and then forward to the Finish. Establish the position physically using the checkpoints, then create the visual image.

Putting the Still Frames Together
SIDE VIEW

○ ○

READY POSITION   THE TURN   CONTACT POINT   FINISH POSITION

Executing the Forehand

Once you have learned the still frames and the checkpoints, you can put them together into a full swing pattern. The four still frames and their corresponding mental images are the key elements you must have to develop superior stroke production. Using them, you will teach your body to execute the motion effortlessly and automatically. Your goal is to execute the swing over and over until you pass through each of the still frames correctly on every repetition. This is called building *muscle memory*.

Building your muscle memory is a three-step process. First, you should practice the forehand swing *without* actually hitting balls. If possible, do this in front of a full-length mirror. Start with one swing, and build up to ten perfect swings. Make sure that you pass through each of the still frames correctly. If you are unsure, stop and refer to the checkpoints. You can also refer to the full stroke sequences at the beginning of the chapter to improve your feel for the overall motion. You may find that the model images of the still frames will spontaneously come to mind, guiding the motion. If you are struggling with a particular aspect of the motion, go back and re-create it physically and visually for yourself. Doing regular practice swings is particularly vital for beginning players.

The second method for creating muscle memory is hitting balls in *controlled drill*. A fundamental principle of visualization training is that it is impossible to develop or correct a stroke by playing games, or even by rallying. To make the process work you must have controlled conditions. This means having the opportunity to hit a stream of well-placed balls, coming at low to moderate speed. Also, the balls in controlled drill should come directly to you, and should not require extensive footwork to reach and set up for.

You can create controlled drill by working with a practice partner, or with a teaching pro, who can also help monitor your progress. However, the best way to work in controlled drill is with a ball machine rented at a club or public tennis center. The advantage of the ball machine is the great precision of the ball placement, something that rapidly facilitates the development of muscle memory.

If you are a beginner, or if at first you find it difficult to execute the entire motion, start in the Turn Position, with the racket already back and the body aligned according to the checkpoints. Once you are able to execute the stroke then begin from the Ready Position, and develop the full motion.

Work in controlled drill until you can hit ten strokes according to the model. As you hit balls, you should also do muscle memory corrections, as explained in the next section. These will allow you to monitor the technical progress of your stroke. When you can hit ten strokes with real precision, increase the speed of the balls, and the number of repetitions.

The next step in controlled drill is to add footwork, or movement to the ball. When the ball does not come directly to you—as it almost never does in a match—your goal is to beat the ball to where it is going and to set up for the stroke as if it had come to you in the first place. There are two crucial aspects to accomplishing this. The first is to turn immediately, before actually moving to the ball. This means getting the shoulders sideways to the net and the racket all the way back. Players who do not prepare first, but simply take off after the ball, often get there in time, but then must rush to finish the backswing. This makes them late at the contact, and, as a consequence, they almost never learn to execute a solid stroke. In addition, without the full shoulder turn, they may lose significant power, even if the racket preparation is correct. This is why it is crucial to turn immediately. With practice, a player may naturally start to spread the racket preparation over the duration of the movement, but this is not necessary, and is virtually impossible to achieve at the beginning. In order to learn correct preparation, the player should start with an immediate, full turn prior to any movement to the ball.

The second step in learning footwork is to move by taking short, choppy steps. The small steps allow you to position yourself precisely to the ball. Players who take large, awkward steps are either too close to the ball at contact, or too far away. Short steps allow you to control the intervals of your movement so that you can position yourself to step parallel, directly into the shot. For the split second of the hit, you should be set, with your weight forward on the front foot. Do not step through the stroke with the back foot, or allow the motion to rotate you off your base. You can analyze your footwork by doing muscle memory corrections as explained in the next section. After the stroke, return immediately to the Ready Position, and slide step back to the center of the court.

As with the basic stroke, develop your footwork working with a ball machine, if possible. Start by moving two or three steps to the ball, and gradually increase the distance. Make your movement to the ball wider and wider until you can cover both corners of the court. As you work on moving to wider balls, you will find that the length of your steps will naturally increase, but that you will come back to the small choppy steps when you reach the ball and set up to step into the shot. Next you should progress to rallies, and finally, match play. The last section of this chapter will show you how to develop and use stroke keys to execute the stroke under competitive pressure. If you find that your execution is breaking down in matches, go back to controlled drill until your confidence and consistency return.

The third technique for developing your muscle memory is pure visualization, or practicing visualizing your stroke away from the court. As explained in the Introduction, you can practice visualizations by allocating specific practice time to sit down and do them, or you can simply make use of spare moments in the course of your day. Whenever you find your mind turning to your tennis game, take the opportunity to work on your visual models. Visualize yourself executing a perfect forehand. In your mind's eye, see yourself pass through each still frame, and make sure the checkpoints are correct. Work up to ten visual repetitions. Supplement this visual work by watching video of high-quality forehand stroke execution. You can use existing instructional tapes and also tape matches of top professional players. The *Visual Tennis* video is designed specifically to enhance this modeling process.

Muscle Memory Corrections

○ ○

Muscle memory corrections are a crucial aspect in the development of a technically sound forehand stroke pattern. Accordingly, they should be a regular part of your work in controlled drill.

What, exactly, is a muscle memory correction? It is a simple procedure that allows you to recognize and correct your errors as they happen, before you can repeat them and they become ingrained in your stroke pattern.

To make a muscle memory correction, you simply freeze at the end of the stroke in your followthrough position. Do not recover for the next shot. Instead, stop exactly where the stroke finished, and be statueman.

From the statueman position, you now compare your actual finish with the checkpoints for the correct Finish Position. How does your stroke compare with the checkpoints for the racket, the hitting arm, the shoulders, and the legs? Note any differences. Now, simply adjust your body and racket from wherever they actually are to the corrected Finish Position. This is a muscle memory correction. The muscle memory correction process allows your muscles literally to feel the difference between what you did and what you were trying to do, that is, to execute the swing correctly according to the model.

By making a muscle memory correction after the stroke, you increase the probability that your *next* stroke will be correct or, at least, approximate the model more closely. By doing regular corrections in controlled drill, you will eventually bring the two in line, so that the stroke follows the model on a consistent basis. You will also find that you are hitting the stroke solidly and effortlessly. If, on the other hand, you hit a lot of forehands in controlled drill or rallies without making corrections, you will reinforce your errors, creating tendencies that will be more difficult to correct later. In developing your muscle memory corrections, you should make extensive use of video. By watching videos of your actual stroke production, you will not only see how you are deviating from your model, you will develop a much clearer image of the model stroke itself.

The following sequences show you how to do muscle memory corrections for the most common types of forehand errors: errors in the position of the racket or the hitting arm, and errors in leg position. Using the checkpoints, you can diagnose other errors that differ from the ones shown below. These examples, however, will show you how the muscle memory correction process actually works on the court.

Muscle Memory Corrections: Racket and Hitting Arm

The following sequences demonstrate the three most common errors in the followthrough on the forehand. Each error involves incorrect positioning of the racket and the hitting arm. By freezing in the statueman position at the end of the stroke, these errors can be corrected before they become ingrained in your stroke pattern. To make the correction, compare the actual position of your arm and racket to the checkpoints for the correct forehand finish. Then simply reposition the racket as shown below.

      The first error shown is a short swing, or the lack of a complete followthrough. Typically, this will result in hitting long, and in a lack of consistent topspin. The second error is releasing the wrist at contact. This results in a loss of body leverage and thus power, and also in a loss of control of shot direction. The third error is turning the racket over. Although this sometimes produces heavy topspin, it also causes great inconsistency and a high percentage of unforced errors. By correcting these, and any other errors, in controlled drill, you will develop a consistent, technically superior followthrough, a central component in hitting the forehand well.

STATUEMAN
Short Followthrough and Correction

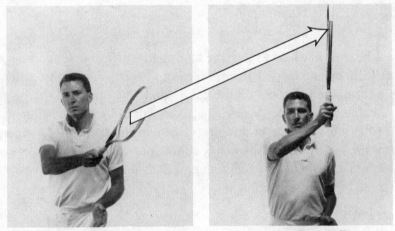

ERROR: SHORT FOLLOWTHROUGH   CORRECTED FINISH POSITION

STATUEMAN
Wrist Release and Correction

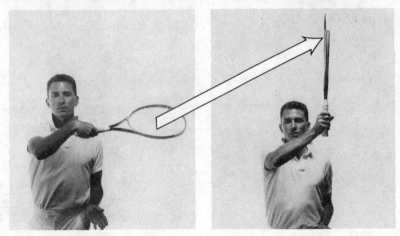

ERROR: WRIST RELEASE AT FINISH   CORRECTED FINISH POSITION

STATUEMAN
Turning the Racket
Over and Correction

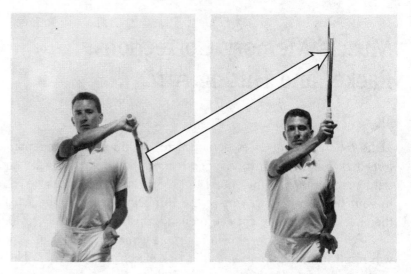

ERROR: RACKET HEAD TURNED OVER AT FINISH   CORRECTED FINISH POSITION

Muscle Memory Correction:
Leg Position

The sequence below shows the most common error in leg position at the finish of the forehand: finishing with an open stance. This error is caused either by an incorrect step to the ball, or by allowing the swing to rotate the front foot off the court during the course of the swing. In either case, the player finishes the shot with an open stance, makes late contact with the ball, and loses both body leverage and control of the shot. To correct this error, freeze in the statueman position. Now, referring to the checkpoints for the legs at the finish, simply adjust your body to the correct position. Note that the tips of the toes of *both* feet should be parallel along a straight line, with the knees slightly flexed, as shown in the second photo of the correct position.

STATUEMAN
Open Stance
and Correction

ERROR: OPEN STANCE AT FINISH POSITION   CORRECTED FINISH POSITION

44

KEYING THE FOREHAND

The purpose of the visualization process is to help you develop a forehand that will be reliable, especially under pressure. Most forehand errors result from a breakdown in basic stroke production. If you watch most players, you will see that the level of stroke execution varies considerably from one ball to the next. When the stroke deviates too far from the correct swing pattern, it breaks down, producing an error.

The visualization training system overcomes this fundamental problem by creating a system of personal *stroke keys*. A stroke key is a single visual element of the stroke pattern that is used to activate the *entire* stroke. The process for using a stroke key is simple: in the split second before hitting the shot, the player visualizes *the image of the key*. By holding this mental image in mind, the player triggers the execution of the whole stroke pattern. The key functions as a kind of mental blueprint, which the body then naturally follows. By mastering the still frames, and learning to execute the forehand stroke in controlled drill, you have laid the groundwork for creating your stroke keys.

The following section outlines a half dozen of the most effective keys for this stroke. Determining which of these keys are most useful for your game is something you must do by trial and error. Theoretically, an image of any part of the stroke could be an effective key. Each of the four still frames is a potential key, as are the individual *checkpoints* for each of the still frames. By working in controlled drill, you must determine whether a given key consistently activates your forehand stroke. If it does, the key is an *active key*.

In my experience, the single most powerful key for the forehand is the image of the Finish Position. Thus, the image of the Finish Position is the first forehand key presented here, and the first key you should test for yourself. First, do a practice swing and freeze in the Finish Position. Make sure each of the checkpoints is correct. Now close your eyes, and visualize yourself in the correct Finish Position. You will probably see yourself in your mind's eye from over your shoulder and from slightly behind, and also, from about the waist up. This is what I call the *player's perspective*. The image of the Finish Position, as well as several of the other keys, are therefore presented from this viewpoint. As you see the image of the finish in your mind, give it as much detail as possible. This image will now become the blueprint for the execution of the correct stroke.

Now, test the key by working in controlled drill. As the oncoming ball approaches, visualize your image of the Finish Position. Hold the picture in your mind's eye, and as you swing, make *the real racket* overlap the image. You will find that the image will function as a magnet, attracting the racket to the correct Finish Position. As you hit balls, work to make the racket and the image correspond as precisely as possible. Monitor your success in doing this with muscle memory corrections. Until you work with the finish key, there is no way to understand how powerful it is, or how consistent it can make your stroke execution. Once the key is solid in controlled drill, you can test it in rallies and then matches.

You may want to experiment with slight variations of the finish key by focusing on one or more of the checkpoints, such as the double bend arm position, or the wrist at eye level, etc. Test each variation in the same fashion described above. As the oncoming ball approaches, visualize the image of the key. Make your real arm, racket, wrist, etc., overlap the image. Do this for ten to twenty balls. If the stroke pattern improves, then this key is *active* for you, and you should add it to your stroke key chart.

As noted in the introduction, a second major source of unforced errors on any stroke is the tendency to overhit the ball, usually in the attempt to hit a winner. When most players have an opening to win a point, they regularly try to hit the ball too hard, often ending up with an unforced error. This is particularly true on the forehand, which most players consider to be their best weapon. The tendency can be attributed to overexcitement, but also to a fallacy in the way players think about the stroke. It is a common assumption that using more muscle will lead to more ball velocity, and hence the belief that to hit a winner you should hit the ball as hard as possible.

In terms of the physics of the stroke, the truth is completely the reverse. When players overhit the forehand, they associate the higher level of muscle tension they feel in their arms with a harder shot. But if we examine what is happening to the racket at contact, we can see this is not the case. When a player muscles the ball, he tenses his arm and takes a shorter stroke, concentrating on the contact point and reducing the length of the followthrough. But with this tense, short followthrough, the racket is actually *decelerating* as it approaches the ball, since the swing comes to a stop shortly after contact. Because it is the speed of the racket head that imparts velocity and spin, the use of excess muscle creates the opposite effect from what the player intends. It slows down the racket at contact. Without topspin to give the shot an arcing flight, he is also more likely to hit the ball either into the net or out of the court. Unfortunately, our nerve endings do not extend into the racket head. Thus, there is no way for the players to feel directly what is happening at the moment of ball contact. We can feel only what is happening in our hitting arm, not in the racket head itself. Too many players make the mistake of associating muscle tension in the arm with racket head speed.

In reality, by relaxing and stroking to the correct Finish Position, the player ensures that the racket head acceleration will be maximized. This will, in turn, maximize both pace shot velocity and ball rotation. The role of the followthrough in generating power explains the effortless quality that we associate with the strokes of the great pro players. They hit the ball with tremendous velocity, yet their strokes seem fluid and effortless. This is because they rely on good technical execution, rather than on brute force. They maintain a certain level of relaxation, even under great pressure. This allows their rackets to do the work through natural acceleration. When players ask me how to hit the ball harder, the answer is to relax, and execute the stroke. If the Finish Position is correct, then the racket will generate pace naturally and automatically. Beyond this, additional velocity comes from the legs, as will be explained below.

In addition to the Finish Position key, there are two other basic keys for the forehand. These are the image of the turn and the image of the contact point. If you have difficulty with either of these aspects of the stroke, these keys will eliminate the problem. For some players, they may also prove as effective, or even more effective, than the Finish Position in activating the entire stroke pattern. You should experiment with them in controlled drill to determine if this is true for your game.

Finally, there are three supplemental forehand keys. The first shows you how to key the stroke by visualizing the palm of the hand as the face of the racket. For many players, this key will be helpful in eliminating wrist release at contact, and also, in coordinating the proper roles of the shoulders and hitting arm throughout the stroke. The last two keys are more advanced. The first demonstrates the role of the legs in generating additional power. The second key shows you how to create additional topspin by hitting up on the ball more sharply at contact. Experiment with these keys when the bio-mechanics of the basic stroke pattern are solid.

One important aspect of developing your keys is correlating specific keys with your most frequent errors. The ultimate benefit of the stroke key system is that it teaches every player to understand the types of mistakes he makes and how to correct them on the court. What are your tendencies, and what are the counteracting keys? This process is called *tendency analysis*. For example, if you or your teaching pro discover that your contact is consistently late, you will want to work extensively with the image of the contact point as a key. Or, similarly, if you find that you are having difficulty with the preparation of the racket and/or the body position, you should create a key using the image of the Turn.

As you experiment with developing and refining your keys, systematize them into a personal stroke key chart. In the last section of the book, I include a sample chart to serve as a model. The chart has two parts. First it identifies up to four keys that are usually active on the stroke. Second, it provides tendency analysis. In this section, the player lists his typical errors, and with them the counteracting keys he has developed for each tendency.

One of the great difficulties most players face in actually playing the game is knowing what to think on the court. Often they are consumed by negative thoughts about their own game, about their opponent, or about strategic situations that occur in the course of a match. Worse, their minds often wander to something else entirely—to virtually any topic other than tennis. It is important in tennis that the mind be continually focused during play. Great players concentrate almost instinctively. As noted, some previsualize their shots spontaneously, others, have made it into a conscious technique. Unfortunately, this is rarely the case below the top levels of the game. Many players do not realize that they are not really concentrating, and most teaching pros have no systematic approach for teaching mental focus.

The stroke key system provides a framework for overcoming these problems and creating concentration on the court. Since it is based on a series of images, the entire system is *nonverbal*. As noted in the Introduction, the game simply moves more quickly than a human being can think, at least in words. The images of stroke keys provide a method for producing consistently high-quality tennis because they can flow through the mind at the same speed the game is actually played on the court.

The learning procedure for creating your stroke keys is identical to that for mastering the still frames. First, establish the position physically, referring to the checkpoints that accompany the image. Next, close your eyes and create an image of the position in your mind's eye, giving it as much detail as possible. Notice how the position feels physically, and make the image and the feeling correspond in your mind. Now test the key in controlled drill. As the ball approaches, hold the image of the key in mind; as you swing, make your racket, hitting arm, shoulders, etc., overlap the image of the key. Determine whether the key is active, and if so, add it to your personal stroke key chart.

Keying the Forehand: The Finish Position from the Player's Perspective

○ ○ ○ ○ ○ ○ ○ ○ ○ ○ ○ ○ ○ ○ ○ ○ ○ ○ ○

As discussed above, the image of the Finish Position is the single most effective key to activate the forehand for most players. If the finish is correct, then the entire stroke pattern is usually correct as well. The finish key also eliminates the tendency to overhit on the forehand, and actually maximizes pace and topspin.

The finish image is presented from the player's perspective—how most players actually see themselves in their mind's eye, from over the shoulder, and slightly behind. Note the checkpoints for the stroke: the wrist at eye level, the hitting arm in the double bend position, the shaft of the racket vertical to the court, and the face of the racket perpendicular to the left shoulder. Establish the position physically, then create the image. Test the key in controlled drill.

Keying the Forehand: The Turn Position from the Player's Perspective

○ ○ ○ ○ ○ ○ ○ ○ ○ ○ ○ ○ ○ ○ ○ ○ ○ ○ ○

One of the most difficult problems for any player to correct is an error in the Turn Position. If the Turn is incorrect, it leads to late contact and poor body leverage. Doing muscle memory corrections at the end of the stroke does not reveal or correct this error. The solution is to key on an image of the

Turn. By holding the image of the Turn at the start of the stroke, the player can guide his body and racket into the correct position, quickly correcting a serious technical flaw.

The image shown here is, again, from the player's perspective, over the shoulder, the way that most players visualize themselves. Note that the shoulders are fully turned. The racket head points straight back to the back fence. The shaft of the racket is parallel to the court, and the face of the racket is perpendicular. The arm is in the double bend position. Establish the position physically, and create the mental image. Now test the key in controlled drill.

Keying the Forehand: The Contact Point from the Player's Perspective

○ ○ ○ ○ ○ ○ ○ ○ ○ ○ ○ ○ ○ ○ ○ ○ ○

Although the correct finish will usually produce an early Contact Point, some players find that the image of the contact itself is a more effective key for the forehand. If late contact is a tendency, this key will correct it.

Early contact ensures that the stroke will have the maximum body leverage, and hence, shot velocity. Early contact is also what gives the shot a solid and effortless feeling. Again, the key is created from the player's perspective. Note the checkpoints. First, the racket is well in front of the front leg. The wrist is slightly laid back with the elbow in toward the waist. The shaft of the racket is horizontal, and the face of the racket is perpendicular to the court. Establish the position physically and then create the mental image. Test the key in controlled drill.

Keying the Forehand: The Palm of the Hand Is the Face of the Racket

○ ○ ○ ○ ○ ○ ○ ○ ○ ○ ○ ○ ○ ○ ○ ○ ○

THE SEQUENCE ABOVE SHOWS THE IMAGE OF THE PALM AS THE FACE OF THE RACKET AT THE TURN, THE CONTACT POINT, AND THE FINISH POSITION.

One of the most common technical errors on the forehand is releasing the wrist at contact. This tendency detaches the racket head from the body and destroys the power and consistency of the shot. To correct this tendency, visualize the palm of the hand as the face of the racket. This will keep the wrist slightly laid back throughout the swing. Establish the physical position for each of the three frames above, then create the visual image. Test the key in controlled drill by visualizing a still image of the palm at one of the three key frames, or a mini-movie of the entire motion.

Keying the Forehand: Using the Legs for Power and Topspin

○ ○ ○ ○ ○ ○ ○ ○ ○ ○ ○ ○ ○ ○ ○ ○ ○ ○

If you have developed your forehand properly, you should already be getting leg leverage in your shot. This key will show you how to increase it to its full potential.

The front thigh muscle, or the quadricep, is the strongest muscle in the body. When you bend the knees at the step to ball, you coil the quadricep as if it were a spring. As the racket sweeps forward to the Contact Point, the spring uncoils into the shot. By increasing your knee bend, you can increase this uncoiling effect at contact. This increases the acceleration and the brushing action of the racket face on the ball. The result is more pace and topspin. The stroke will feel effortless and the swing will still be smooth and relaxed, but will have noticeably more velocity and ball rotation. Create the physical position shown above by maximizing your knee bend at the step to the ball. Then create the visual image. Test the key in controlled drill.

Keying the Forehand: Hitting Up on the Ball for Topspin

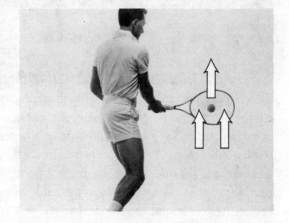

○ ○ ○ ○ ○ ○ ○ ○ ○ ○ ○ ○ ○ ○ ○ ○ ○ ○

The forehand swing pattern you have developed is designed to produce topspin automatically. If the racket face is vertical to the court at contact, the strings will brush the back side of the ball, causing the ball to rotate over itself. But the ability to hit up on the ball, and therefore the amount of topspin generated, can be increased using this key. As you improve and face players who hit with more velocity, you will find you need additional spin to control the ball and keep it in the court. The only change required to alter the amount of spin is a slight increase in the steepness of the swing plane. The racket face should remain vertical, but move more sharply upward at contact, as the arrows show. Establish the physical position shown above, and create a visual image of hitting up, with the racket brushing the face of the ball. Test the key in controlled drill.

Variation:
The Circular Backswing

○○○○○○○○○○○○○○○○○○○○

1
READY POSITION

2   **3**
PATH OF THE CIRCULAR BACKSWING

4
THE TURN

Advantages of the Circular Backswing: As noted at the start of the forehand chapter, the circular backswing, at least in theory, generates more racket head speed because the racket is in continuous motion along the path of a circle, rather than stopping at the end of the backswing. Instead of taking the racket back directly along a line to the Turn Position, the path of this backswing is in a semicircular loop. As the shoulder turn starts, the racket moves *upward* from the Ready Position along a curved arc (Frame 2). At the highest point, the tip of the racket is roughly even with the top of the head (Frame 3). The racket then descends along the same arc to the Turn Position (Frame 4). Thus the backswing has traced the circumference of a half circle. Some players will develop this larger looping motion naturally, and execute the forehand well using it. Also, players who were taught the loop initially, but find that it is now causing problems, may find it easier to correct the flaws than to change to a straight backswing.

Similarities to Straight Backswing: Note that during the course of the circular motion, the elbow stays bent, tucked in toward the waist. At the completion of the Turn (Frame 5), the racket is in virtually the same position as in the straight backswing; it has simply arrived there by an alternate route. Once the Turn is complete, the forward motion of the stroke follows the same path as in the straight backswing. Thus the stroke has the same general technical characteristics and bio-mechanical simplicity as the straight backswing forehand, producing natural body leverage, power, and topspin.

Keying the Circular Backswing:
The Position of the Hitting Arm

○○○○○○○○○○○○○○○○○○○○○○○○○○○○

 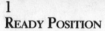  

1
READY POSITION

2
START OF THE TURN

3
THE TURN

The key to executing the circular backswing correctly is maintaining the correct hitting arm position throughout the motion. The common tendency, however, is for the arm to get out away from the body, so that it is moving independently from the body and the swing is too large. The result is a backswing that takes too long to execute, contact that is late, and a stroke hit primarily with the arm, and with little body leverage.

The antidote to this tendency is to key the stroke on the hitting arm position. As the arrows in the sequence above show, the elbow should stay in, pointing toward the waist throughout the backswing. In effect, the backswing revolves around the pivot point of the elbow, so that at the completion of the turn, the hitting arm is in the perfect double bend position. The player is now in position to execute the rest of the stroke according to the classical forehand model presented above.

Create your own circular backswing key using the images above. The key can be an image of the arm position at any point in the backswing, or a mini-movie of the entire motion. Test the key in controlled drill, and, once it is solid, in rallies and match play. In addition to the specific keys for the circular backswing, the remainder of the stroke should be keyed using the same images for the straight backswing forehand. Experiment with these, as well as the backswing keys, in creating your forehand stroke key chart.

Variation:
The Closed Face Backswing

○○○○○○○○○○○○○○○○○○○○○○○○○○○○○○

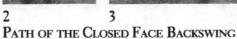

1
READY POSITION   **PATH OF THE CLOSED FACE BACKSWING**

2   **3**

4
THE TURN

Differences from the Circular Backswing: As in the circular backswing, the closed face backswing has a semicircular arc, but with two differences. First, the racket head is tilted downward in the Ready Position (Frame 1). Second, for the first two feet, the racket starts back along a straight line (Frame 2). Only then does the racket start to move upward on a circular path (Frame 3). At the highest point, the racket head is at shoulder level. From here it starts downward on the same arc, until the completion of the Turn (Frame 4). At the Turn, the face of the racket is still tilted downward. It will automatically become vertical as it approaches the ball. Players looking for more power and spin can consider trying the closed face backswing, as well as players struggling to correct problems with the classic loop.

Advantages of the Closed Face Backswing: The first advantage of the closed face backswing is that it is more compact than the classical loop. With the closed face, the racket comes up to about shoulder level at the highest point, versus the classical loop, which reaches the top of the head or higher. This means that the stroke can be executed more quickly, because the racket travels a shorter distance. Yet because the motion is still circular, the acceleration is continuous, and thus produces increased racket head speed and shot velocity. The second advantage of the closed face loop is that it produces more topspin. This is because, at the completion of the backswing, the racket head is lower (Frame 4). This produces a steeper swing plane, more brushing effect at contact, and thus, more ball rotation.

Keying the Closed Face Backswing:
Closing the Racket Face

○ ○

1
READY POSITION

2
START OF TURN

3
THE TURN

The key to executing this backswing is achieving the correct racket face position at the start of the stroke. Although Ivan Lendl keeps his racket vertical in the Ready Position, a player working on this variation can ensure that the motion starts correctly by waiting for the ball with the racket face already closed, at about forty-five degrees to the court. As the arrows show, the face remains closed as the racket goes back (Frame 2), then up and around, and down to the Turn (Frame 3). Note that as the racket starts up on the circular part of the motion, the elbow moves up and away from the waist. However, if the face remains closed, the elbow will automatically be forced back in toward the waist at the completion of the backswing. This will ensure the preservation of body leverage in the stroke.

Use the images above to create your own key, or keys, for the closed face backswing. An active key can be an image of the racket face closed at the start, at any part of the motion, or a mini-movie of the entire motion. It could also be the correct double bend position of the arm, with the elbow in to the waist and the face still slightly closed at the completion of the backswing.

Test each key in controlled drill, and once it is solid, move on to rallies and match play. In addition to the backswing keys noted here, the remainder of the stroke should be keyed on the same images as the straight backswing forehand. Compile your keys into your forehand stroke key chart.

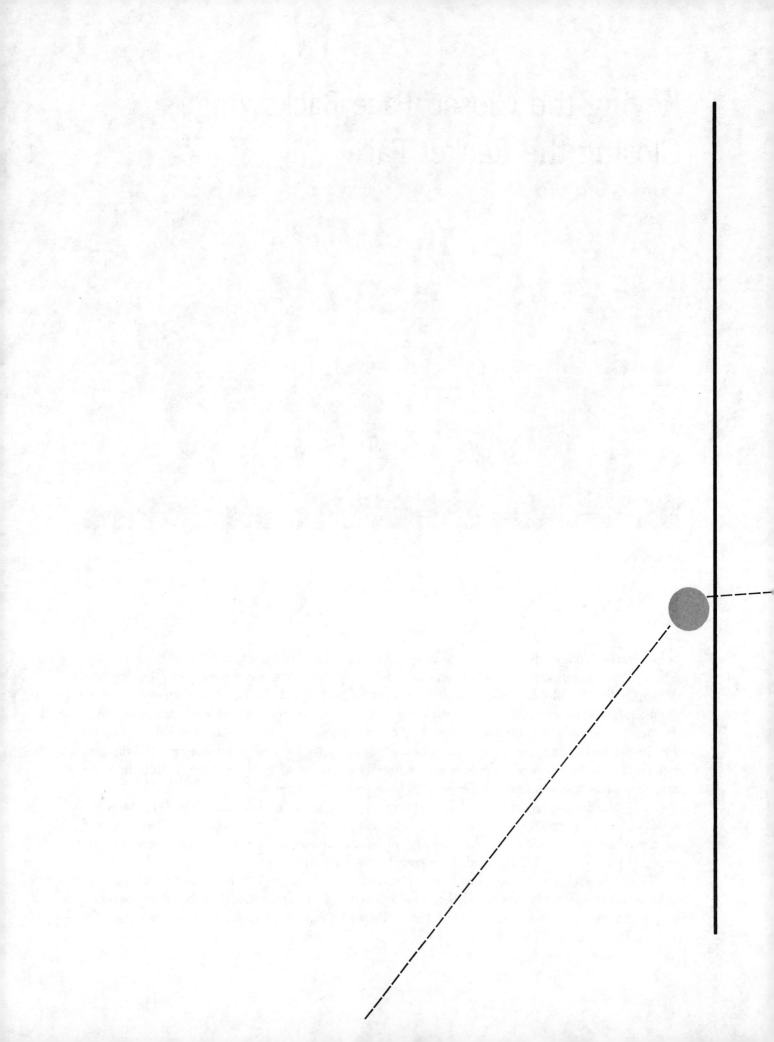

THE
BACKHAND

As we have seen, it is possible to play classical tennis with either a one-handed or a two-handed backhand. The question every player has to answer is: which stroke will work best in my game?

In discussing the relative advantages of the two strokes, there are two factors to consider. The first consideration is strategic: which backhand is better suited to my style of play? The second consideration is practical: which backhand can I develop and learn to execute most quickly?

Turning first to the strategic question, there are pluses and minuses on both sides, but generally, the one-handed is better suited for attacking tennis, and the two-handed for baseline play.

Although it is possible to volley well with two hands once you are at the net, the two-handed backhand is, usually, a liability on approach shots and in the mid-court game. This is due to the difficulty of hitting low volleys with two hands, and also, the greater difficulty of hitting with slice. Without slice, two-handers are simply less effective on short balls, low balls, approach shots, and first volleys. In these situations, to get the racket head under the ball, the two-hander has to push the ball up into the air, making a weaker and more defensive shot.

The one-handed backhand, on the other hand, is supremely versatile in the attacking game. A one-handed player can take a low ball, or a short ball, hit a sliced approach shot, and follow it to the net. Because of this ability to hit with underspin, as well as the slightly extended reach, the one-handed backhand is also superior on low volleys and half-volleys. The key to playing attacking tennis is to be able to make these difficult half-court volleys, and these require the use of slice to get the ball up over the net and down inside the baseline.

Two-handed players who are determined to slice effectively are forced to develop a separate one-handed shot. Bjorn Borg and Mats Wilander, two of the greatest two-handers of all time, both developed a one-handed slice to overcome the limitations of the two-handed style. But this alternative is difficult for most players. The bio-mechanics of the two strokes are so different that going back and forth between them requires tremendous mental and physical flexibility. Few players who try to combine the two-handed drive with a one-handed slice ever succeed in producing both backhands consistently. Thus, throughout the history of the game, it is not surprising to discover that the great serve and volley players have all played their backhands with one hand.

Conversely, almost without exception, the great two-handed players in the modern era have been baseliners. First, the two-handed shot, if properly executed, is a more powerful shot. At best one-handed players can hit their backhands with about 85 or 90 percent of the pace on their forehands. But the two-hander can be hit with at least as much and sometimes with more power than the forehand. Therefore, a two-hander will generally have more ball velocity on the backhand side than his one-handed counterpart. This makes the two-handed backhand a formidable shot in baseline rallies and on return of serve. It is not unusual for the backhand to become the stronger side for a two-hander, forcing his opponents to play to his forehand side.

Second, it is easier to hit the two-handed shot with topspin, and to vary the amount of topspin. The relative ease of producing spin makes the two-handed shot at least the equal of the one-hander for passing shots. Also, because the stroke is produced with bio-mechanics that are similar to those of the forehand, high balls are much less of a problem for the two-hander. With two hands, the player can hit up through a high ball with relative ease, producing good pace and heavy topspin. The one-handed player, by com-parison, is forced to play most high balls with slice, and cannot usually generate the same pace as a two-hander on a comparable ball, let alone generate topspin. While it is true that the bio-mechanics of the two-handed shot make it slightly more difficult to set up for running balls, the great two-handed champions, as well as thousands of successful junior players, have proved that the reduced reach of the stroke is not a major drawback, as was once commonly thought. Actually, in a backcourt rally, all other factors being equal, the two-handed player usually has the advantage.

This is not to imply that one-handed players cannot play outstanding baseline tennis. We need look no further than Ivan Lendl to see how effective the one-handed backhand can be from the backcourt. Steffi Graf, already one of the greatest women players of all time, is another excellent example of a one-handed backhand player who wins from the backcourt. Given the success of these two players, it is hard to conclude that the one-handed backhand is always deficient in the backcourt. In fact, the one-handed style has some clear advantages of its own in backcourt play. The one-handed stroke can be hit with slice, hit flat, or hit with topspin, all with only slight variations in the basic stroke pattern. This means that in a backcourt rally the one-handed player can vary the pace and spin of the ball at will, upsetting the rhythm and neutralizing the pace of a two-handed opponent.

Just as it is impossible to claim that the one-handed backhander never wins from the baseline, it is also incorrect to assume that two-handed players never win at the net. Jimmy Connors has always mixed volleys effectively into his overall game. Chris Evert has done the same thing at various points in her career. Bjorn Borg, the quintessential baseliner, played serve and volley tennis in capturing his last Wimbledon title, beating off the challenge of the young John McEnroe. And the South African champion Frew McMillan, one of the greatest volleyers of all time, volleyed with two hands on *both* sides.

For most players, however, these types

of detailed strategic comparisons are less important than a second, more practical consideration: which shot can be developed most easily and most rapidly, and which shot will be most consistent and most effective for the individual player? In American junior tennis, the last fifteen years have seen the two-handed backhand become the dominant choice. There is a reason for this trend: for junior players, and for many adults as well, the two-handed shot is *far* easier to learn initially, and can become a reliable stroke, at times, almost immediately. The fact is that most junior players do not have the strength to hit the one-handed backhand effectively until the age of fourteen or even sixteen. With players starting at earlier and earlier ages, this can mean years of frustration trying to develop the one-handed shot. The two-handed backhand, however, requires less strength than the one-handed backhand, or the forehand for that matter, and is therefore far easier for many players to learn.

Another major drawback in learning with one hand is that a one-handed player must master hitting the ball with slice as well as with topspin. Without slice, a one-handed player is almost defenseless against a high ball to the backhand, or against a short low ball. Once mastered, the variety the slice offers becomes a strength, but attempting to master two spins simultaneously is a serious difficulty for a beginning player. Usually, it is necessary to spend months solidifying either the slice or the topspin drive before the other can be added, and this protracted learning process puts the one-handed player at a decided disadvantage in the interim.

From the point of view of the teaching pro, it is usually counterproductive to teach the one-handed backhand to juniors. Occasionally, of course, there are junior players who are exceptions, and who have the extra strength or superior timing to develop a one-handed stroke at an early age. Also, junior players who have the inclination (and the volleying ability) to play attacking tennis should consider either persevering with the one hand or switching from two hands to one as soon as they are physically strong enough. But generally junior players at all levels are better off with a two-handed backhand because it will allow them to enjoy playing the game in the shortest period of time, and allow them to play it well. For most juniors, it is simply ridiculous to spend five or six years trying to play tennis without a backhand.

The same argument can be made for many beginning adults, particularly women. Because the two-hander is so much quicker to learn, and because it requires less strength, beginning women pick it up as quickly as the forehand. Often this is also true for experienced women players who have struggled for years with ineffective one-handed backhands. After hitting only a few balls with the two-handed shot, many find their backhand problems are solved. Any woman player who has consistent problems on the backhand side should definitely experiment with switching to two hands.

In some cases this same line of reasoning applies to male players. However, it is generally more difficult for adult men to learn with two hands. First, the two-handed backhand is technically very similar to a left-handed forehand. Therefore it requires that a player be at least somewhat ambidextrous, so that his left arm and left hand can guide the stroke. Second, it requires greater physical flexibility, because of the additional body rotation required to hit the two-handed shot, something we will discuss in detail later. While rarely a stumbling block for junior or women players, these two requirements usually make it harder for a man to develop the shot. For whatever reasons, most adult men tend to be more right-side dominant, and also, considerably less flexible than women. Thus, for beginning men, the two-handed backhand is an awkward, stiff shot, unlikely ever to become a flowing, natural stroke. The same is true for an experienced male player with a weak backhand who decides to experiment with the two-hander. Although it is worth trying two hands, the majority of men will progress more quickly toward a natural stroke if they learn to hit with one hand.

Occasionally, of course, the reverse is true. The final decision must be made based on the combined judgment of the student and the teaching pro. Usually, after a period of experimentation, the choice becomes obvious. As a rule of thumb, I start junior players by showing them the two-handed backhand. I start beginning men with one hand, and beginning women with two. If they do not make initial progress, then it is definitely worth experimenting with the alternate style, until it becomes clear which will work best for the given player.

If you choose the one-handed style, it will be necessary to learn both the topspin drive and the slice. To be a complete one-handed player, it is necessary to have both shots. In the beginning stages, however, it is impossible to learn them simultaneously. Rather, a player should work to solidify one as a basic backhand, and add the other only when this has been achieved. The question then becomes, which should you learn first? In my teaching experience, I have found most players are more comfortable learning the flat or moderate topspin drive. For this reason, I have presented the one-handed topspin drive as the basic model for learning the bio-mechanics of the stroke, and the one-handed slice as a variation.

A significant percentage of players, however, will have the natural tendency to come under the ball. There is no way to predict which will work for you. The best way is to start with the model for the topspin drive, and then see what happens. If, in learning the topspin drive, you or your pro detect that you are tending naturally to hit under the ball, then you should recognize this tendency, switch gears, and develop the slice.

Although the majority of players will gravitate to the flat or topspin drive, for the minority who have a natural affinity for slice, it may actually be an advantage. With slice you can play the ball anywhere on the court, whether it is high or low, deep or short. With the one-handed topspin drive, it is extremely difficult to come over these balls. Also, the slightly more compact nature of the slice stroke makes it possible to hit balls when you are rushed, when you are unable to set up completely, or when you are forced to hit on the run. Again, because of the compact and versatile nature of the stroke, it is usually the basic pattern on return of serve. Ken Rosewall, who had one of the most beautiful and most effective backhands ever, hit with moderate slice and never found it necessary to come over the ball. However, I have found that it is virtually impossible, initially, to teach a player to hit the slice one-handed backhand—unless he or she shows a natural affinity for the stroke.

Most one-handers will be more comfortable with the topspin drive, and learning this first has advantages of its own. First, it can usually be hit with more pace. Because it can also be hit with varying degrees of topspin, it is superior for passing shots, and also, because of the superior pace, for forcing the play in baseline rallies.

Turning to the one-handed models themselves, some students of the game will notice that both the topspin and underspin strokes presented here have straight backswings. The objection may be raised that most experienced players do not use a straight backswing. Rather, they bend the elbow up at the start of the backswing, raising the racket head to about shoulder level first, and dropping it down only as the racket approaches the contact point. It is true that, for an advanced player, this loop backswing may offer an advantage. The looping motion helps add a rhythmic quality to the stroke, and also, it makes the motion more continuous, which may in turn produce slightly more racket head speed. Trying to perfect the loop backswing from the outset, however, is almost certain to arrest, or more likely, prevent, development of a sound overall stroke.

The problem with teaching the loop backswing is that it tends to result in an "elbow lead." This means that the player's elbow remains bent too long so that it moves through the swing *ahead* of the racket. The elbow lead is, in fact, probably the most common technical flaw among one-handed players. With the elbow leading the stroke, the contact point can never be correct. Instead it will always be disastrously late, well behind the front edge of the body. From this contact position, a player has insufficient leverage to execute a solid stroke, and produces instead a weak, uncontrolled shot.

One of the most crucial aspects of *either* one-handed shot is that the arm must be straight at contact so that the ball is played in front of the body. With the straight backswing this is much easier to achieve. The arm is in the correct hitting position already, and it is simply a matter of keeping it that way throughout the course of the swing. In contrast, the loop backswing requires that a player move his arm into the hitting position in the midst of the swing.

With all the other factors that a player must control to learn a new stroke, it is asking too much for him to start with his elbow in the wrong position. Having the arm straight at contact is far more important than any small improvement in rhythm or racket head speed stemming from a loop backswing. Usually, a player who learns to hit with the straight backswing will begin to loop naturally, once the mechanics are solid and he is hitting the shot with confidence. But since the difficulties it causes far outweigh its marginal benefits, I have excluded it from my basic models. In this respect, the backhand models are analogous to those for the forehand. Both place the arm in the correct hitting position at the start of the stroke, a position that remains unchanged throughout the movement. This eliminates unnecessary variables and is a key to consistent stroke production. If your natural inclination is toward the two-handed backhand, you will avoid, at least initially, the problem of choosing between two variations of the basic stroke. Although, as noted, there are disadvantages to hitting certain balls with two hands, it is at least possible to play everything with the basic two-handed stroke pattern. Depending upon how successful you are playing low balls and short balls, you may eventually experiment with adding the one-handed slice. But this is something mainly for advanced players to consider.

Turning to the two-handed stroke pattern itself, it should be noted that in the model presented here, both hands are used for the *entire* stroke, and remain on the racket handle at the end of the followthrough. It is true that some two-handers let go at the contact point, or shortly thereafter. Borg did this from the beginning, and Jimmy Connors has as well in the latter stages of his career, although, as a younger player, he almost always played the shot with both hands. I think it is crucial for most players to use the full two-handed stroke. In fact a case can be made that Borg's backhand was not a true two-hander, but rather a "one-handed push," since he hit it with an extreme eastern backhand grip, and used the front arm at least as much, if not more than the back arm to generate power. For the true two-hander, as we will see, the back left arm should dominate the swing. This is what makes the shot so effective and easy to learn—it is hit with biomechanics that are very similar to those of a left-handed forehand. Letting go in the middle of the swing confuses the relationship between the front and back arms in making the hit, introduces additional variables that are difficult to control, and adds no appreciable benefit to the effectiveness of the stroke. The two-handed model used here is what I call the "true" two-hander. It is the stroke used by Chris Evert, Mats Wilander, and the young Connors. It will provide you with the most consistent and effective stroke if you choose the two-handed backhand.

In the sections that follow, you will see how to hit both the one-handed and the two-handed backhands using visualization techniques. As discussed, you may need a period of experimentation, working with your teaching pro or coach, to decide which is best for you. But the basic problem most players face on the backhand side is not only deciding how many hands to use, but developing effective stroke production with *either* style. Through visualization you can create a solid technical foundation for either stroke. Some players go through their entire tennis lives living in fear of their backhands. Using the stroke patterns in this book, combined with a little hard work, your backhand can become a shot you look forward to hitting. It could even become the strength of your overall game.

CREATING THE ONE-HANDED TOPSPIN BACKHAND SWING PATTERN

As was the case with the forehand, the heart of the visual approach to learning the one-handed topspin backhand is a series of still frame sequence photos. These sequences will serve as a blueprint for creating your own swing pattern. Through visualization techniques, you will learn a precise *physical* and *visual* model of the stroke.

As with the forehand, the shot is first demonstrated from the front view, and broken down into its component parts. Accompanying this sequence is a description of the general technical characteristics of the stroke. On the next four pages, the stroke is presented simultaneously from both the front and side views. These sequences isolate the four key still frames. The still frames are:

1. **The Ready Position**
2. **The Turn**
3. **The Contact Point**
4. **The Finish Position**

By looking at the overall sequence, you can see how passing through each of the four positions correctly will guarantee that the entire swing pattern is correct. If the swing is correct at the Ready Position, at the Turn, at the Contact Point, and at the Finish Position, it will *have* to be correct at every point in between as well.

Following the same progression as with the forehand, the next section teaches you to master each of these four positions through a series of checkpoints. Then, you will put the still frames together into a complete one-handed topspin backhand swing pattern. The next section shows you how to do muscle memory corrections, eliminating your errors as they occur. Finally, you will learn how to create your own personal system of stroke keys for the one-handed topspin backhand that will allow you to hit the stroke consistently in actual play and under competitive pressure.

1	2	3	4	5
READY POSITION	START OF TURN	THE TURN	STEP TO BALL	START OF SWING

Characteristics of the One-Handed Topspin Backhand FRONT VIEW

○ ○

Grip: The one-handed topspin backhand begins with the classical eastern backhand grip. The grip shift takes place immediately at the Start of the Turn (Frame 2). If you are unsure of the correct backhand grip, it is explained in the grip chapter.

Differences from Forehand: The primary difference between the forehand and the one-handed backhand is that on the backhand the hitting shoulder is *automatically* in front when the body reaches the Turn (Frame 3). On the forehand, the hitting shoulder must rotate ninety degrees to reach the Contact Point. On the backhand, the hitting shoulder is positioned at the front edge of the body *before* the start of the swing. Hence the one-handed backhand is hit with less body rotation. The motion

6
CONTACT POINT

7
START OF
FOLLOWTHROUGH

8
FOLLOWTHROUGH

9
FINISH POSITION

is something like the swinging of a gate on a hinge. The arm and racket are the gate, locked together in one piece, swinging on the hinge of the shoulder, making it vital that the arm and racket stay *straight* throughout the entire motion.

Minimum Use of Wrist: This straight arm position means that the one-handed backhand is hit with a minimum of wrist action. The position of the wrist, once the grip is changed, remains the same throughout the motion. With the arm straight and the wrist locked at the Start of Swing (Frame 5), the contact cannot help but be in front of the body (Frame 6)

Vertical Swing Path: As with the forehand, the one-handed topspin backhand is hit with a vertical swing path. This means the racket face stays perpendicular to the court surface throughout the motion. This vertical position can be clearly seen at the Ready Position (Frame 1), the completion of the Turn (Frame 3), the Contact Point (Frame 6), and the Finish Position (Frame 9).

Natural Topspin and Power: With the racket face vertical, the one-handed player will produce natural topspin. At the Contact Point, the vertical racket face brushes upward along the back side of the ball (Frame 6). This brushing action causes the ball to rotate over itself automatically. An additional source of topspin is the uncoiling of the legs. As the player Steps to Ball (Frame 4), his knees are fully bent. At the Contact Point (Frame 6), the uncoiling happens automatically, continuing through to the Finish Position (Frame 9). This causes increased acceleration of the racket head, and maximizes the brushing effect on the ball. In addition, this uncoiling of the legs, combined with the early contact in front of the shoulder, maximizes body leverage on the ball, creating natural power and shot velocity.

One-Handed Topspin Backhand:
Four Key Still Frames · SIDE VIEW

○ ○

STILL FRAME #1   **STILL FRAME #2**

READY POSITION   **START OF TURN**   **THE TURN**   **STEP TO BALL**   **START OF SWING**

One-Handed Topspin Backhand:
Four Key Still Frames · FRONT VIEW

○ ○

STILL FRAME #1   **STILL FRAME #2**

READY POSITION   **START OF TURN**   **THE TURN**   **STEP TO BALL**   **START OF SWING**

STILL FRAME #3

STILL FRAME #4

CONTACT POINT   START OF FOLLOWTHROUGH   FOLLOWTHROUGH   FINISH POSITION

STILL FRAME #4

STILL FRAME #3

CONTACT POINT   START OF FOLLOWTHROUGH   FOLLOWTHROUGH   FINISH POSITION

67

Still Frame 1
The Ready Position

○ ○ ○ ○ ○ ○ ○ ○ ○ ○ ○ ○ ○ ○ ○

Checkpoints:

1. *The Shoulders:* The shoulders face the net in the Ready Position. The upper body is straight up and down from the waist. The bend is in the knees, not the waist.

2. *The Hitting Arm:* The hitting arm is positioned so that the elbow tucks into the waist. This is the same as for the forehand. Wait with the forehand grip.

3. *The Racket:* The racket is slightly below waist level. It points directly at the net. The face of the racket is perpendicular to the court surface.

4. *The Legs:* The legs are shoulder width apart, or slightly wider. The knees are flexed, and the weight is slightly forward on the balls of the feet.

Establish the Ready Position physically using the checkpoints, then create the mental image.

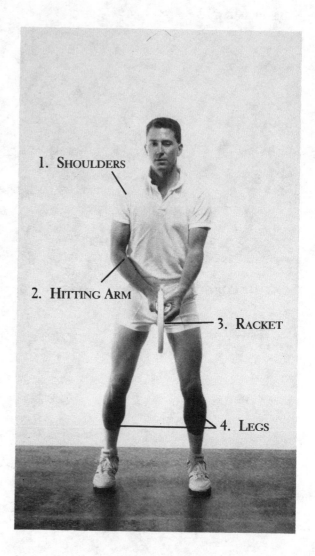

1. SHOULDERS

2. HITTING ARM

3. RACKET

4. LEGS

Still Frame 2
The Turn Position

○ ○ ○ ○ ○ ○ ○ ○ ○ ○ ○ ○ ○ ○ ○ ○

Checkpoints:

1. The Shoulders: The shoulders have rotated ninety degrees, and have moved from parallel to perpendicular to the net. The right shoulder is pointing directly at the net, and the head is turned slightly to follow the oncoming ball.

2. The Hitting Arm: The hitting arm is straight. The racket hand is positioned in line with the middle of the back leg. This naturally positions the racket below waist level.

3. The Racket: The racket has traveled straight back along a line until it is pointing at the back fence. The racket is horizontal, or parallel, to the court. The butt of the racket is visible to the opponent. The *face* of the racket is still perpendicular to the court.

4. The Legs: Both feet have pivoted sideways and are pointing to the side fence. The weight is on the *left* pivot foot, and the right toes are used for balance. The knees are still flexed.

Move from the Ready Position to the Turn. Establish the position physically using the checkpoints, then create the mental image.

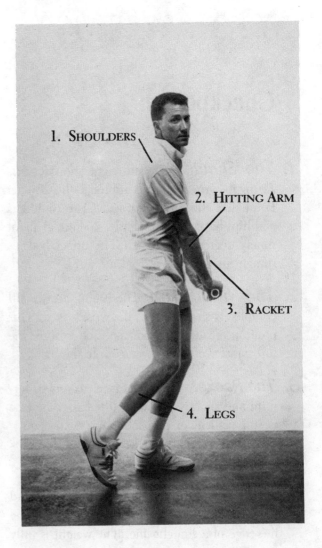

1. SHOULDERS

2. HITTING ARM

3. RACKET

4. LEGS

Still Frame 3
The Contact Point

○ ○ ○ ○ ○ ○ ○ ○ ○ ○ ○ ○ ○ ○ ○ ○

Checkpoints:

1. The Shoulders: The right shoulder has swung the arm and racket around to the Contact Point, like the hinge of a gate. The shoulders and hips have rotated slightly, and are at about ninety degrees to the net. The upper body is straight up and down from the waist.

2. The Hitting Arm: The hitting arm is still completely straight, with the wrist locked. This position creates early contact, and ensures the full transfer of body leverage into the ball.

3. The Racket: The racket face has moved forward and slightly upward to the ball. The face is still vertical or perpendicular to the court. This ensures that the racket will brush the back of the ball, creating topspin.

4. The Legs: The right foot has stepped forward to the ball, so that the toes are parallel, along the edge of a straight line. The weight is fully forward on the right foot, and the knees have started to uncoil.

Move from the Ready Position through the Turn to the Contact Point. Establish the position physically using the checkpoints, then create the mental image.

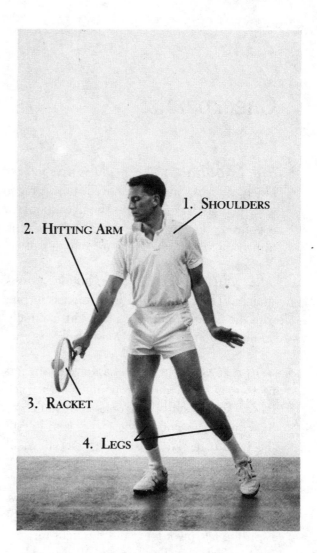

1. SHOULDERS

2. HITTING ARM

3. RACKET

4. LEGS

Still Frame 4
The Finish Position

○ ○ ○ ○ ○ ○ ○ ○ ○ ○ ○ ○ ○ ○ ○ ○

Checkpoints:

1. The Racket: The racket has accelerated upward to the Finish Position. The wrist is at eye level. The racket is straight up and down, with the butt pointing straight down at the court. The racket has swung about forty-five degrees past perpendicular to the net.

2. The Hitting Arm: The arm is still straight, as it has been throughout the motion. It is now in line with a line drawn across the front of the shoulders. The wrist remains locked, and has released at impact or through the course of the followthrough.

3. The Shoulders: The shoulders have rotated slightly at the finish, opening up a maximum of forty-five degrees to the net. The upper body remains straight up and down from the waist.

4. The Legs: The weight is fully forward on the right front foot. The player has come up on his left rear toes for balance. The knees have uncoiled into the ball, but remain slightly flexed.

Move from the Ready Position through the Turn to the Contact Point to the Finish Position. Establish the position physically using the checkpoints, then create the mental image.

1. RACKET

2. HITTING ARM

3. SHOULDERS

4. LEGS

Putting the Still Frames Together
SIDE VIEW

○ ○

READY POSITION   **THE TURN**   **CONTACT POINT**   **FINISH POSITION**

Executing the One-Handed Topspin Backhand

Once you are familiar with each of the key still frames and the checkpoints, you can start putting them together into practice swings. The sequence above shows you how to do this. Start in the Ready Position, move to the Turn, then to the Contact Point, and finally, the Finish Position. Make sure the checkpoints are correct at each stage. As you develop the stroke, practice the correct swing over and over, until you can execute the entire swing, automatically passing through each of the still frames correctly. This is called building muscle memory.

As noted in the forehand chapter, it is literally impossible to build good muscle memory in actual play, or even just rallying. This is true regardless of your level of play. To apply the principles of visualization properly, you must work extensively in controlled drill, hitting a steady stream of low to moderate speed balls. These balls must be well placed, and hit directly to you, so that no running is necessary to set up for the stroke. Controlled drill can be arranged by renting a ball machine at a club or public tennis center. You can also work with a practice partner, taking turns feeding balls to each other. Or you can work with a teaching pro, who can not only feed you the balls, but can help monitor your progress.

The purpose of controlled drill is to learn how to hit the stroke pattern precisely and correctly, building muscle memory and confidence. An initial goal is to hit ten one-handed topspin backhands exactly according to the model. As explained in the next section, muscle memory corrections will help you monitor your level of success in executing the stroke correctly. As soon as you are able to execute ten strokes, you can gradually increase the speed of the balls you hit, and/or the number of repetitions.

The next step in controlled drill is adding footwork, or movement to the ball. Since the ball rarely comes directly to you in a match, your goal is to beat the ball to wherever it is going and to set up for the stroke, as if it actually had come to you in the first place. As with the forehand, there are two aspects to accomplishing this. The first is making an immediate turn. This means getting the shoulders sideways to the net and the racket all the way back *before* starting the movement. Players who do not prepare first, but simply take off after the ball, often get there but rarely have time to finish the backswing once they arrive. This makes them late at the contact, and, as a consequence, they do not develop a solid, consistent stroke. Also, without the full shoulder turn, they may lose power, even if the racket preparation is correct. With practice, a player may naturally start to spread the racket preparation over the duration of the movement, but this is not necessary, and is virtually impossible to develop intentionally.

The second step in learning footwork is taking short, choppy steps. The small steps allow you to position yourself precisely to the ball. At contact, players who take large, awkward steps are invariably too close or too far away. Short steps allow you to control the intervals of your movement so that you can position yourself to step directly into the shot. For the split second of the hit, you should be set, with your weight forward on the front foot. Do not step through the stroke with the back foot, or allow the motion to rotate you off your base. You can analyze your footwork by doing muscle memory corrections as explained in the next section.

As with the basic stroke, develop your footwork working with a ball machine, if possible. Start by moving two or three steps to the ball, and gradually increase the distance. Make your movement to the ball wider and wider until you can cover both corners of the court. As you work on moving to wider balls, you will find that the length of your steps will naturally increase, but that you will come back to the small choppy steps when you reach the ball and set up for the shot. Now progress to rallies. If the stroke breaks down, return to controlled drill to reestablish the correct swing pattern.

You should also increase your muscle memory by doing practice swings away from the court. If possible, do this in front of a full-length mirror. Start in the Ready Position and execute a practice swing in super slow motion. Make sure that you pass through each of the still frames, and that the checkpoints are correct. If you are uncertain, take the time to stop and compare them with the models. Do ten perfect swings. Try to do this every day, and build up to twenty-five or even fifty swings.

A second component of building muscle memory is to practice visualizing the one-handed topspin backhand. To do this, repeat the process described above *visually*. Start in the Ready Position and see yourself execute a practice swing. Again, make sure that, in your mind, you see yourself passing through each of the still frames, and that the checkpoints are correct. Start with ten perfect swings, and as above, work up to twenty-five or fifty. If you wish, you can also do physical practice swings as you visualize.

You can do your visualization practice in other ways. Anytime you find your mind drifting to your tennis game take the opportunity to practice a few visualizations of the shot. You can do this at work, or even if you are caught in traffic. Any spare moments can be converted to working on your backhand, even if you are nowhere near a court.

The second component of off-court visualization is watching videos of good technical backhands. The *Visual Tennis* video provides you with these images, as do *The Winning Edge* and other instructional tapes.

Muscle Memory Corrections

○ ○

As with the forehand, a central aspect in the development of the one-handed topspin backhand is the process of muscle memory correction. Doing muscle memory corrections should be a regular aspect of your work in controlled drill.

Muscle memory corrections allow you to recognize and correct your errors *as they happen*, before they have the chance to repeat themselves and become habitual.

On the backhand, do your corrections as follows: at the end of the stroke, stop and freeze your body in your followthrough position. Literally freeze like a statue—do not recover after the stroke.

From the statueman position, compare your actual finish with the checkpoints for the correct Finish Position. How does your finish compare? Note the difference. Now, move your body and racket from wherever they actually are to the correct Finish Position according to the checkpoints. This process allows your muscles literally to feel the difference between what you did and what you were trying to do, execute the model stroke with a correct finish.

By making a muscle memory correction after the stroke, you dramatically increase the probability that your next backhand will be correct, or will approximate the model stroke more closely. By doing a series of corrections in controlled drill, you will eventually bring the two in line so that your stroke follows the correct pattern on a consistent basis. Conversely, if you hit a lot of backhands without correcting, you end up reinforcing your errors, and creating bad habits that will be more difficult to correct later. In working on your corrections, you should make extensive use of video. By watching video of your actual stroke production, you will not only see how you are deviating from your model, you will develop a much clearer image of the model stroke itself.

By using the muscle memory correction process, you will see radical improvements in your stroke pattern. When you are working in controlled drill, stop after approximately every five balls and do a complete muscle memory correction. As you progress, you will note that your corrections will be smaller and smaller, and that your stroke begins to follow the model more consistently. You will also notice that you are hitting the ball solidly and effortlessly.

The following sequences show you how to do muscle memory corrections for the most common one-handed topspin backhand errors. These are errors on the followthrough in the position of the racket and hitting arm, and errors in the leg position. You can diagnose your own particular errors if they differ from these by using the checkpoints.

Muscle Memory Corrections:
Followthrough

These three sequences demonstrate the three most common errors on the one-handed topspin backhand followthrough.

The first error is stopping the swing short, or the lack of a complete followthrough. The second error is the release of the wrist at contact, causing the face of the racket to turn over, rather than stay vertical. The third error is the elbow lead, in which the elbow remains bent throughout the stroke, causing late contact.

Each of these problems can be rectified by muscle memory corrections. By making these corrections in controlled drill you will develop a consistent, full followthrough, which is crucial in learning to hit the stroke consistently.

STATUEMAN
Short Followthrough
and Correction

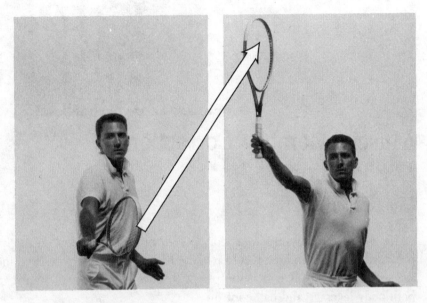

ERROR: SHORT FOLLOWTHROUGH   CORRECTED FINISH POSITION

STATUEMAN
Wrist Release
and Correction

ERROR: WRIST RELEASED AT FINISH   CORRECTED FINISH POSITION

STATUEMAN
Elbow Lead
and Correction

ERROR: ELBOW LEAD AT FINISH POSITION   CORRECTED FINISH POSITION

Muscle Memory Correction:
Leg Position

This sequence shows the most common error in leg position on the one-handed topspin backhand. It is caused either by an incorrect step to the ball, or by rotating the front foot off the correct position during the swing. The result is that the player finishes with an open stance, making late contact, and losing both body leverage and ball control.

To correct, freeze in the statueman position. Now, referring to the checkpoints for the legs, adjust to the correct position. The tips of the toes of both feet should be parallel along a straight line, as shown in the second photo.

STATUEMAN
Open Stance
and Correction

ERROR: OPEN STANCE AT FINISH POSITION   CORRECTED FINISH POSITION

KEYING THE ONE-HANDED TOPSPIN BACKHAND

The goal of the visualization learning process is to develop a one-handed topspin backhand that will be consistently effective, especially under the pressures of actual play. If you observe most players' backhands, you will notice how the majority of their errors result from breakdowns in technical stroke production. Their stroke varies in the level of execution from one ball to the next. Eventually, it deviates too far from the correct pattern and breaks down, producing an error. Visualization offers a solution to this fundamental cause of inconsistency.

The crucial step in developing a reliable backhand is creating your own personal system of *stroke keys*. A stroke key is a single element taken from the stroke pattern that is used to activate the entire stroke in actual play. The process for using a key is simple: in the split second before actually hitting the shot the player *visualizes the key*. By holding this mental image in mind, the player triggers the correct execution of the entire stroke pattern.

Mastering the key still frames and learning to execute the stroke in controlled drill and in rallies are prerequisites for developing your stroke key system. Through these preliminary steps, the player develops the muscle memory that makes the use of the keys possible. Then, by using the image of the key on the court, the player triggers this reservoir of muscle memory. This gives the player a reliable method for hitting effortless, technically superior strokes in match play. The development of keys is a personal process, and must be done by trial and error over time. Theoretically, there are a dozen or more keys that could be effective. In reality, each individual will find certain keys produce the stroke almost as if by magic, while others do not.

For the one-handed topspin backhand, an active key could be the image of any one of the four still frames, or an image of any one of the checkpoints. However, as with the forehand, the single most effective key is usually an image of the Finish Position, since any stroke that finishes correctly was, in all probability, correct on its way to the finish as well.

To create the finish key, follow this procedure: do a swing and freeze in the Finish Position, making sure the checkpoints are correct. Now close your eyes and visualize yourself in that position. What I have found is that the vast majority of players will see themselves in their mind's eye from over their *opposite* shoulder. (For the backhand, this means the left shoulder.) Also, they will see themselves from about the waist up. Once you have created this image in as much detail as possible, it will become your blueprint for the stroke.

Now you are ready to test the key. Start first in controlled drill. As the oncoming ball approaches, hold your image, or blueprint, of the Finish Position in your mind. As you swing, put your actual racket directly over the *image* of the racket in the blueprint. Strive to make them overlap as perfectly as possible. With practice, you will find that the blueprint image will function almost as a magnet, attracting the racket to the correct Finish Position. Try this process for ten to twenty balls. Now evaluate the result: how well did you hit the ball? If the key produces consistently high-quality backhands, then it is an *active key* for you. Repeat the test in the rally. If it continues to be active, you are ready to try out the key in match play. You may also want to experiment with slight variations of the image, focusing, for example, on one of the checkpoints, such as "wrist at eye level," or "straight hitting arm," etc.

In addition to the Finish Position, I have provided images of the two other most effective keys for the majority of players. These are images for the Contact Point, and for the Turn, both seen from the player's perspective. If you are having difficulty with late contact, or the preparation of the racket, you should work with these keys. Some players find they are more active than the image of the Finish. Create these keys by the same process described above.

Finally, I have provided two additional keys. The first is for maintaining a straight hitting arm position throughout the course of the swing, a critical element in the one-handed backhand. The second is for increasing the roll of the legs in the shot. This key will help any player increase pace and spin once the basic bio-mechanics are solid.

As outlined for the Finish Position key above, the learning procedure for creating your stroke keys is identical to that for mastering the still frames. First, establish the position physically, referring to the checkpoints that accompany the image. Next, close your eyes and create an image of the position in your mind's eye, giving it as much detail as possible. Notice how the position feels physically, and make the image and the feeling correspond in your mind. Then test the key in controlled drill. As the ball approaches, hold the image of the key in mind, and as you swing, make your racket, hitting arm, shoulders, etc., overlap the image of the key. Once the key is solid in controlled drill, you can move on to rallies and match play.

The final step in developing your key system is tendency analysis. Each player should understand the types of mistakes he usually makes and how to correct them on the court. This means recognizing which keys counteract your most frequent types of errors.

As you experiment with developing and refining your keys, systematize them into your own stroke key chart, as explained in the final section. The chart has space for you to identify the active keys for your one-handed topspin backhand. It also has space to chart your individual tendencies, and the counteracting keys for each tendency. You can take the stroke key chart on the court with you and refer to it in matches during game changes.

As mentioned in the forehand chapter, one of the major problems most players face in matches is knowing how to think on the court, and specifically, how to maintain concentration. The stroke key system provides a method for achieving continuous focus. As noted, the game moves more quickly than human beings can think in words. Stroke keys provide a method for maintaining concentration and producing consistently high-quality tennis, because the key images can flow through the mind at the same speed the game is actually played on the court. Experiment with the keys presented here, and develop others either on your own, or in conjunction with your teaching pro. Test them in controlled drill, rallies, and in match play, and add them to your chart, updating it regularly.

Keying the One-Handed Topspin Backhand: The Finish Position from the Player's Perspective

○ ○

As discussed, the image of the Finish Position is usually the most powerful single key for the backhand. This is because the entire stroke pattern must be correct in order to produce a correct finish. A common question asked by students is: why is followthrough so important, if the ball is already off the strings at the Contact Point?

The answer is that the Finish Position determines *how* the racket is moving at the Contact Point, and thus the nature of the hit. The racket face must be accelerating upward and outward toward the Finish Position to create power and spin at contact. Note the checkpoints: the racket shaft is vertical, the arm straight with the wrist at eye level, and the swing has gone about forty-five degrees past perpendicular to the net. Establish the position physically, and create the mental image. Test the key in controlled drill.

Keying the One-Handed Topspin Backhand: The Turn Position from the Player's Perspective

○ ○

A vital aspect of the stroke is the correct execution of the Turn. The correct Turn positions the body and the racket to make a solid stroke. Many players have backhand problems that stem from an incorrect or incomplete Turn. These can be overcome by creating the key shown here. Again, this image is from the player's perspective—how most players tend to see themselves in their mind's eye. Note several key elements. The shoulders are fully turned. The racket is all the way back with the arm straight and the racket hand in the middle of the back leg. The racket face is *vertical* to the court. Establish the physical position and create the mental image. Test the key in controlled drill.

Keying the One-Handed Topspin Backhand: The Contact Point from the Player's Perspective

○ ○ ○ ○ ○ ○ ○ ○ ○ ○ ○ ○ ○ ○ ○ ○ ○ ○ ○

This image is designed to create a key for the Contact Point from the player's perspective. Although a correct Finish Position will usually result in correct contact, many players find it effective to key on the image of the Contact Point itself.

There are several important points to note. First, when the contact is well in front of the front leg the body leverage on the ball is maximized. Second the arm is straight, and the racket is horizontal to the court. From this viewpoint you can also see how continuing the swing outward and upward will result in the racket face brushing the ball, creating topspin. Establish the physical position and create the mental image. Test the key in controlled drill.

Keying the One-Handed Topspin Backhand: Straight Hitting Arm Throughout Swing

○ ○

THE ARROWS SHOW HOW THE HITTING ARM IS STRAIGHT AT THE TURN, THE CONTACT POINT, AND THE FINISH POSITION.

A straight hitting arm eliminates the danger of an elbow lead, and ensures that you achieve maximum body leverage on the ball. Note that the arm is already straight at the turn. From there it is only a matter of maintaining the correct alignment at the Contact Point and at the Finish Position. Establish each of the three positions shown above physically, and create the mental images. The key can be an image of the arm at any of the three positions, or a mini-movie of the entire motion. Test the key in controlled drill.

Keying the One-Handed
Topspin Backhand:
Using the Legs
for More Power and Topspin

○ ○

**AT THE STEP TO BALL, MAXIMIZE YOUR KNEE BEND
TO INCREASE BALL VELOCITY AND TOPSPIN.**

If you watch Ivan Lendl hit topspin backhands, you may have been struck by the tremendous leverage he gets from his legs. He has so much knee bend, occasionally he actually touches his back knee down on the court. Few players have the strength and flexibility to go down this far, but every player, once the basic stroke pattern is reliable, should try to maximize his own knee bend. By going down as far as possible and shifting the weight fully to the front (right) leg, you increase the uncoiling action of the legs into the ball at contact. This adds racket head speed and increases the natural brushing action of the strings on the ball. The result is significant additional ball velocity and topspin. Establish the position physically and create the mental image. Test the key in controlled drill.

Variation:
The One-Handed Slice Backhand
SIDE VIEW

○ ○

1	2	3	4	5
READY POSITION	**START OF TURN**	**THE TURN**	**STEP TO BALL**	**START OF SWING**

Grip: The one-handed slice backhand is hit with the same classical eastern grip as the topspin shot. Again, the grip shift takes place immediately at the start of the Turn (Frame 2). Refer to the grip chapter if you are not sure that you are using the correct grip.

Similarities to Topspin Backhand: Like the topspin version, this shot is hit with the arm straight and the wrist locked. Also, the right hitting shoulder is already in front at the completion of the Turn. The arm and racket are like a one-piece gate swinging on the hinge of the shoulder (Frame 5 through 9). The Contact is well in front of the front leg (Frame 6). Again, there is far less body rotation than on the forehand.

Differences from Topspin Backhand: The two variations of the one-handed backhand differ on two key points. First, to achieve underspin, rather than topspin, the slice backhand is hit with the racket face *slightly open*, rather than perpendicular to the court (Frame 6). Second, the backswing is slightly *higher* (Frame 3), than the topspin shot. Instead of starting below the ball, the slice backswing is made at the level of the ball, or slightly above (Frame 4). If the ball is high or low, the racket is raised or lowered accordingly. From this position, the racket face comes through the ball on a straight line, allowing the racket head to impart natural slice.

6
CONTACT POINT

7
START OF
FOLLOWTHROUGH

8
FOLLOWTHROUGH

9
FINISH POSITION

Generating Slice: To create slice, the racket must move through the Contact Point with the face slightly open, about thirty degrees to the court surface. Visualize the ball as an orange, and the face of the racket as a knife. Now, use the knife to slice off the bottom diagonal third of the ball. This will cause the strings to bite as they slide under the ball, making the ball rotate *backward* under itself, with underspin, or slice. This slicing action can be clearly seen in Frames 5 through 7. Unlike a topspin groundstroke, the slice is not hit with a vertical swing plane. However, as with a topspin forehand or backhand, the angle of the racket face to the court is set by the completion of the Turn, and then *remains unchanged* throughout the course of the swing. Compare this at the Start of Turn (Frame 2), with the Finish Position (Frame 9). This gives the shot a technical simplicity characteristic of the classical style.

Natural Power and Spin: Once the face of the racket is properly set, the underspin will be generated automatically in the course of the swing. Early contact ensures that the body weight transfers naturally into the shot. As with the case of the topspin backhand, the uncoiling of the legs will generate additional racket head speed, and additional spin and shot velocity. At the Step to Ball (Frame 4), the legs are fully coiled. At the Contact Point (Frame 6), they have released slightly into the ball, maximizing the player's body leverage on the shot.

Keying the One-Handed Slice Backhand: The Angle of the Racket Face

○ ○

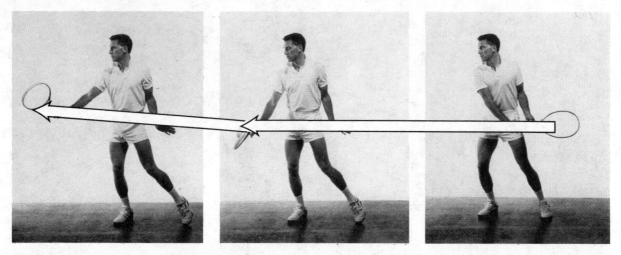

THE ANGLE OF THE RACKET FACE IS SET AT THE TURN, AND REMAINS CONSTANT THROUGH THE SWING, AT THE CONTACT POINT, AND AS THE FOLLOWTHROUGH STARTS.

The key to executing the slice variation of the one-handed backhand is to set up the racket face correctly at the completion of the Turn (Frame 1). The face should be set open at about thirty degrees to the court. The level of the racket head should be at the level of the ball, or slightly higher. Once the angle is correctly set, it remains unchanged throughout the stroke, at the Contact Point (Frame 2), and at the start of the followthrough (Frame 3). Aside from this difference, the bio-mechanics of the slice swing pattern are virtually identical with the topspin variation. The arm is straight throughout the swing, and the Contact Point itself is well in front of the front leg. Note, also, that the racket face has moved outward along the line of the shot, and only then starts upward to the Finish. It is common for players to attempt to swing sharply downward in an attempt to create slice. But this kind of radical, chopping motion will result in late contact, a loss of body leverage and pace, and a tendency for the ball to float. Instead the racket face moves through the ball on a line as shown by the arrow above. The slice is the automatic consequence of this swing plane.

Use the images above as the basis for your keys on the slice backhand. Follow the visualization process described at the start of the chapter to create an image for each of the three positions shown above. As with the topspin variation, your key can be any of the three individual frames, or a mini-movie of the entire motion. Test your keys in controlled drill, then move on to rallies and finally match play. In keying the slice backhand, you should also experiment with the keys for keeping the arm straight and increasing the knee bend presented in the section on the topspin backhand.

Do the off-court visualization work for the slice variation, just as you did in developing topspin.

CREATING THE TWO-HANDED BACKHAND SWING PATTERN

The following section demonstrates the two-handed backhand in a series of still frame photos. These sequences are the blueprint you will use to create your own swing pattern for the shot. As is the case with the forehand and the one-handed backhand, they provide the images for learning a precise *physical* and *visual* model of the stroke.

First, the stroke is broken down into its component parts from the front view, and the general technical characteristics of the stroke are described. Then, the two-handed stroke is shown simultaneously from the front and side views, and the four key still frames are isolated. As with the other groundstrokes, these four still frames are:

1. **The Ready Position**
2. **The Turn**
3. **The Contact Point**
4. **The Finish Position**

Looking at the overall sequence and the four key still frames, it is obvious that if the swing is correct at each of these points, it will be correct for the course of the whole swing as well.

Once the key frames are identified, the next section teaches you how to master each of these four still frames through a series of detailed checkpoints.

Then, the following section shows you how to put the still frames together into a smooth, continuous stroke pattern. Following this, you will see how to do muscle memory correction for the two-handed backhand, correcting your mistakes as they happen. Finally, you will see how to create your own system of stroke keys. These will allow you to execute the shot effortlessly and automatically even under competitive pressure.

1
READY POSITION

2
START OF TURN

3
THE TURN

4
STEP TO BALL

5
START OF SWING

Characteristics of the Two-Handed Backhand FRONT VIEW

○ ○ ○ ○ ○ ○ ○ ○ ○ ○ ○ ○ ○ ○ ○ ○ ○ ○

Grip: The two-handed backhand is hit with *two* forehand grips. The right-hand forehand grip is maintained, and a second forehand grip is added on top with the left hand. The two hands are together, touching, but not overlapping, on the racket handle (Frame 2). This should be your grip in the Ready Position. An alternative is to shift the right hand to a backhand grip, making possible the later development of a one-handed slice backhand. Both variations are demonstrated in detail in the grip chapter.

Differences from One-Handed Backhand: The bio-mechanics of the two-handed shot are radically different from the one-handed. On the two-hander, the *left* arm is the hitting arm. The left hitting arm and the left shoulder dominate the swing, with the right arm adding additional, but secondary support. Thus, the two-handed shot is technically almost identical to a *left-handed* forehand. It relies on rotating the left shoulder and the left hitting arm forward to the contact (Frames 5, 6, and 7), unlike the one-handed shot, in which the right, *front* shoulder dominates the swing.

Minimum Use of Wrist: The position of the left hitting arm on the two-hander is the same

6
CONTACT POINT

7
START OF
FOLLOWTHROUGH

8
FOLLOWTHROUGH

9
FINISH POSITION

as the right hitting arm on the forehand. This means the arm is in the double bend position, with the elbow in toward the body, and the wrist slightly laid back. The arm and wrist are already in this position in the Ready Position (Frame 1). This then remains unchanged throughout the stroke, with the wrist still laid back at the Finish Position (Frame 9).

Vertical Swing Path: The two-handed backhand is hit with the racket face vertical to the court surface throughout the course of the swing, as with the forehand and the one-handed topspin backhand. The racket face is perpendicular to the court in the Ready Position (Frame 1), at the Turn (Frame 3), at the Contact Point (Frame 6), and at the Finish Position (Frame 9). This simple vertical swing path eliminates wrist and arm movement as variables in the stroke, and is a major factor in the ease of learning the two-handed backhand, and in executing it consistently.

Natural Topspin and Power: With the racket face vertical to the court as described above, the player who hits a two-handed backhand will produce topspin simply by executing the swing. The topspin is generated by the rotation of the shoulders, the upward path of the swing, and the uncoiling of the legs. At the Contact Point (Frame 6), the shoulders are rotating forward. The racket face brushes up the back side of the ball, causing the ball to rotate over itself automatically. At the Step to Ball (Frame 4), the knees are fully coiled. The knees release into the ball at the Contact Point (Frame 6), increasing the acceleration of the racket, the brushing of the strings on the ball, and hence the amount of topspin. This leg leverage, when combined with early contact and the full rotation of the body, also creates great natural power and shot velocity.

Two-Handed Backhand:
Four Key Still Frames · SIDE VIEW

○○○○○○○○○○○○○○○○○○○○○○○○○○○○○○○

STILL FRAME #1   **STILL FRAME #2**

READY POSITION   START OF TURN   THE TURN   STEP TO BALL   START OF SWING

Two-Handed Backhand:
Four Key Still Frames · FRONT VIEW

○○○○○○○○○○○○○○○○○○○○○○○○○○○○○○○

STILL FRAME #1   **STILL FRAME #2**

READY POSITION   START OF TURN   THE TURN   STEP TO BALL   START OF SWING

CONTACT POINT   START OF   FOLLOWTHROUGH   FINISH POSITION
                     FOLLOWTHROUGH

STILL FRAME #4

STILL FRAME #3

CONTACT POINT   START OF   FOLLOWTHROUGH   FINISH POSITION
                     FOLLOWTHROUGH

91

Still Frame 1
The Ready Position

○ ○ ○ ○ ○ ○ ○ ○ ○ ○ ○ ○ ○ ○ ○

Checkpoints:

1. *The Shoulders:* The shoulders face the net in the Ready Position. The upper body is straight up and down from the waist. The bend is in the knees, not the waist.

2. *The Hitting Arm:* The hitting arm is positioned so that the elbow tucks into the waist. The hands are together with two forehand grips.

3. *The Racket:* The racket is slightly below waist level. It points directly at the net. The face of the racket is perpendicular to the court surface.

4. *The Legs:* The legs are shoulder width apart or slightly wider. The knees are flexed and the weight is slightly forward on the balls of the feet.

Establish the Ready Position physically using the checkpoints, then create the mental image.

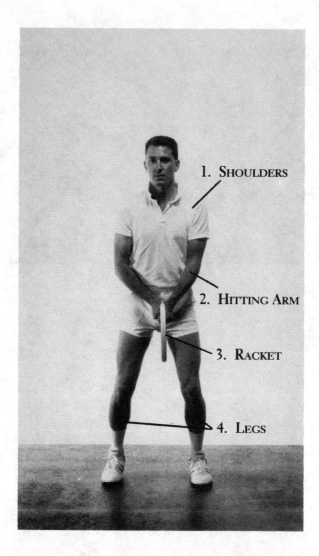

1. SHOULDERS

2. HITTING ARM

3. RACKET

4. LEGS

Still Frame 2
The Turn Position

○ ○ ○ ○ ○ ○ ○ ○ ○ ○ ○ ○ ○ ○

Checkpoints:

1. SHOULDERS

2. HITTING ARM

3. RACKET

4. LEGS

1. *The Shoulders:* The shoulders have rotated ninety degrees, and are now perpendicular to the net. The right shoulder is pointing directly at the net, and the head is turned slightly to follow the oncoming ball.

2. *The Hitting Arm:* The back, left hitting arm is in the double bend position, elbow into the waist, wrist slightly back. The right hand is in line with the middle of the back leg.

3. *The Racket:* The racket has traveled straight back along a line, and points at the back fence. The *shaft* of the racket is parallel to the court surface. The butt of the racket is visible to the opponent. The *face* of the racket is perpendicular to the court.

4. *The Legs:* Both feet have pivoted sideways and are pointing to the side fence. The weight is on the left pivot foot, and the right toes are used for balance. The knees are still flexed.

Move from the Ready Position to the Turn. Establish the position using the checkpoints, then create the mental image.

Still Frame 3
The Contact Point

○ ○ ○ ○ ○ ○ ○ ○ ○ ○ ○ ○ ○ ○ ○

Checkpoints:

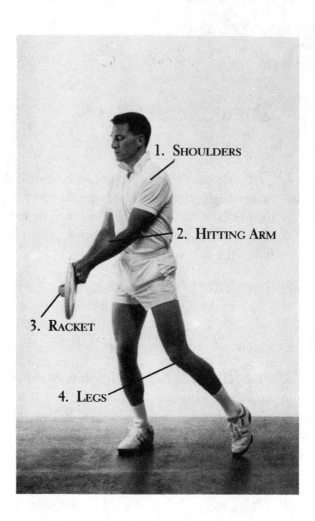

1. **The Shoulders:** The shoulders have rotated back almost halfway to their original position. The back shoulder is solidly behind the arm and racket, absorbing the impact of the hit. The upper body is still straight up and down from the waist.

2. **The Hitting Arm:** The hitting arm is still in the double bend position, and has brought the racket forward to the Contact Point. This position creates early contact and the full transfer of body leverage.

3. **The Racket:** The face has moved slightly upward to contact, creating the brushing effect for topspin. The face of the racket is perpendicular to the court, and the contact is early, in front of the front leg.

4. **The Legs:** The right front foot has stepped forward so the toes are parallel, along the edge of a straight line. The weight is fully forward on the right foot, and the knees have started to uncoil into the ball.

Move from the Ready Position through the Turn to the Contact Point. Establish the position physically using the checkpoints, then create the mental image.

Still Frame 4
The Finish Position

○ ○ ○ ○ ○ ○ ○ ○ ○ ○ ○ ○ ○ ○ ○

Checkpoints:

1. RACKET

2. HITTING ARM

3. SHOULDERS

4. LEGS

1. The Racket: The racket has accelerated up-ward to the Finish Position. The left wrist is at eye level. The shaft of the racket is straight up and down, with the butt pointing directly down at the court. The edges of the frame are per-pendicular to the right shoulder and to the net.

2. The Hitting Arm: The left arm finishes in the double bend position. The elbow is bent, about thirty degrees from horizontal with the court. The wrist has not released, and remains laid back. The *right* arm has collapsed at the elbow.

3. The Shoulders: The shoulders have rotated back fully parallel to the net, as they were in the Ready Position. They have rotated a full ninety degrees through the course of the shot.

4. The Legs: The weight is fully forward on the right front foot. The player has come up on his left rear toes for balance. The knees have un-coiled into the ball, but remain slightly bent.

Move from the Ready Position to the Turn, Contact, and the Finish. Establish the position physically using the checkpoints, then create the mental image.

Putting the Still Frames Together
SIDE VIEW

○ ○

| READY POSITION | THE TURN | CONTACT POINT | FINISH POSITION |

Executing the Two-Handed Backhand

After you master the four key still frames, you can start to put them together into a full swing pattern. The sequence above shows you how. Start in the Ready Position, move to the Turn, then forward to the Contact Point, and, finally, to the Finish Position. Make sure your checkpoints are correct as you pass through each still frame. You are now ready to start building your muscle memory for the stroke. This should be done in three ways.

First, practice the correct swing without actually hitting balls. Do this in front of a full-length mirror if possible. Start with one swing and build up until you can do ten perfect swings, passing through each still frame with the checkpoints correct, without having to think about it.

The second component to building muscle memory is hitting balls in controlled drill. As noted for the other strokes, controlled drill is crucial in establishing correct technical swings. Initially, you must hit balls that have low to moderate pace, and which come directly to you. As you work in controlled drill, do muscle memory corrections to measure your success. Some common corrections for the two-handed backhand are demonstrated in the next section. As with your practice swings, work in controlled drill until you can hit ten strokes with minimal or no correction. You can set up controlled drill practice by renting a ball machine, working with a practice partner or with a teaching pro. When you can hit ten strokes with real precision in controlled drill, you should increase the speed of the balls and the number of repetitions.

The next step in controlled drill is adding footwork, or movement to the ball. Your goal in moving to the ball is to set up as if the ball had come directly to you in the first place. Because it is difficult to hit the two-handed shot with an open stance, the stepup is even more important than with the other groundstrokes. At the split second of the hit, you should be set, with your weight forward on the front foot.

The two key elements in a correct set up are the same as for the forehand, or the one-handed backhand variations. The first is making an immediate turn. This means getting the shoulders sideways to the net and the racket all the way back *before* starting the movement. The second is positioning yourself to the ball with short, choppy steps. An immediate turn means that when you get to the ball you will be ready to hit, rather than having to take time to complete the backswing. Without a good turn, the player will never establish early contact, and will also lose the valuable additional body leverage that comes from the two-handed shot. With experience, players often naturally spread the racket preparation over the course of the movement, but this is not necessary and is virtually impossible to develop initially. It will happen automatically in the course of practice, if at all.

The second aspect to good movement, taking short, choppy steps, allows you to position yourself precisely so that you can step parallel into the shot. Players who take large, awkward steps are usually either too close or too far away from the ball at contact. With short steps, you control the intervals of your movement.

Develop your footwork working with a ball machine, if possible. Start by moving two or three steps to the ball, and gradually increase the distance. Make your movement to the ball wider and wider until you can cover both corners of the court. You will find that the size of your steps will naturally lengthen out, but that you will come back to the smaller steps when you actually approach the ball to set up for the shot. When you feel confident in these variations of controlled drill, progress to rallies. If the stroke breaks down, return to controlled drill to reestablish the correct swing. You can analyze errors in your footwork by doing muscle memory corrections as explained in the next section.

The third aspect of developing good muscle memory is to practice visualizing the stroke away from the court. Visualize yourself hitting a perfect two-handed shot. Again, build your repetitions up to ten, or more. You can practice your visualizations by allocating specific time to do this, or by doing them in your spare moments at work, whenever your mind drifts to your tennis. Another aspect of working visually on your backhand is to watch video. The *Visual Tennis* video is the only instructional tape with extensive images of two-handed stroke production. You can also tape players such as Chris Evert, Mats Wilander, or Andre Agassi. Another good source of video is to tape yourself executing perfect practice swings, or hitting the stroke correctly in controlled drill. Incorporate this into your overall visualization program.

Muscle Memory Corrections

○ ○

Muscle memory corrections are also a basic part of developing an effective two-handed backhand. These corrections should be a regular component of your work in controlled drill.

To review, a muscle memory correction is the simple, powerful procedure that teaches you to recognize and correct your errors *as they happen*, before they can become established habits.

They should be made as follows. At the end of the stroke, stop immediately and freeze in your Finish Position. Literally freeze like a statue—do not recover for the next shot.

From this position, compare your actual Finish Position with the checkpoints for the correct Finish Position. How does your actual position compare with the checkpoints for the racket, the hitting arm, the shoulders, and the legs? Note the difference. Now, simply move your body and racket from wherever they actually are to the correct Finish Position, according to the checkpoints. The process is vital to developing a consistent stroke because it allows your muscles literally to feel the difference between what you really did and what you were trying to do—execute the model stroke with a correct finish.

By making a muscle memory correction after the stroke, you increase the probability that your next stroke will be correct, or will approximate the model stroke more closely. By doing a series of corrections in controlled drill, you will eventually bring your actual stroke in line with the model. Conversely, if you hit a lot of backhands without muscle memory corrections, you reinforce your errors, and deepen a habit pattern that will be more difficult to correct later. In working on your corrections, you should make regular use of video. By watching video of your actual stroke production, you will not only see your errors, you will develop a much clearer image of the model stroke itself.

The following sequences show you how to do muscle memory corrections for the two most common types of errors: errors in the followthrough position of the racket, and errors in leg position. You can diagnose your own particular errors, if they differ, by using the checkpoints.

Muscle Memory Corrections: Followthrough

These three sequences demonstrate the most common errors in the followthrough on the two-handed backhand.

The first error is making too short a swing, resulting in an incomplete followthrough. This causes a loss of ball control due to lack of topspin, and also reduced pace. The second error, releasing the racket with the left hand, causes the loss of the natural body leverage coming from the left side. It also will cause the two-handed player to have difficulty controlling the direction and depth of the shot and produce many unnecessary errors. The third error is breaking the wrists at contact, causing the racket face to turn over rather than remain vertical. When the wrists break, the player tends to hit the ball late, again losing power. In addition, the sudden change in the direction of the racket head makes it hard to control the amount of spin and the trajectory of the shot.

Each of these problems can be rectified by muscle memory corrections. Freeze in the statueman position and examine the position of your actual finish, and, by using the checkpoints, reposition the racket as shown. By making these corrections in controlled drill, you will develop a consistent, full followthrough.

STATUEMAN
Short Followthrough and Correction

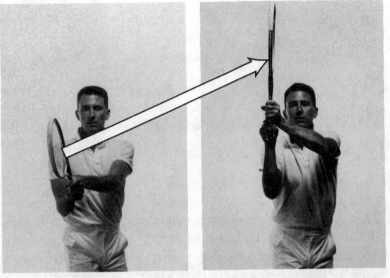

ERROR: SHORT FOLLOWTHROUGH   CORRECTED FINISH POSITION

STATUEMAN
Releasing the Left Hand and Correction

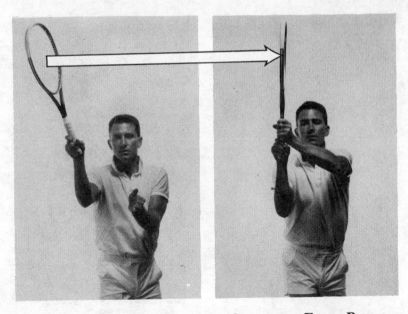

ERROR: RELEASING THE LEFT HAND   CORRECTED FINISH POSITION

STATUEMAN
Releasing the Wrists
and Correction

ERROR: RELEASING THE WRISTS   CORRECTED FINISH POSITION

Muscle Memory Correction:
Leg Position

This sequence shows the most common problem in leg position on the two-handed backhand: finishing with an open stance. This error results either from an incorrect step to the ball, or from rotating off the front foot during the course of the swing. The result is that the contact is late behind the front edge of the body. This means a loss of body leverage, shot velocity, and ball control.

      To correct this error, freeze in the statueman position. Now, referring to the checkpoints for the legs if necessary, adjust to the correct position. The tips of the toes of both feet should be parallel along a straight line, with the knees slightly flexed, as shown in the second photo.

STATUEMAN
Open Stance
and Correction

ERROR: OPEN STANCE AT FINISH POSITION   CORRECTED FINISH POSITION

KEYING THE TWO-HANDED BACKHAND

Once you have developed your muscle memory and are able to hit the two-handed backhand in controlled drill, you can move forward and develop your system of personal stroke keys. The purpose of the stroke key is to allow you to hit the two-handed backhand consistently in match play.

As is the case for the other groundstrokes, the image of the Finish Position is likely to be the most effective key for the two-handed backhand. Again, if the finish of the stroke is consistently correct, there is a very good chance that the entire stroke will be correct as well. The Finish Position key is the first key presented below.

Also included are the keys for the Turn and the Contact Point. If you find you have difficulty preparing correctly for the stroke, then you should work with the image of the Turn. Similarly, if you are taking the ball late, or there is an error in your position at contact causing you to lose power or ball control, experiment with the correct image of the Contact Point. Some players may also find that these keys are more effective than the Finish Position in activating the overall stroke.

The learning procedure for creating your stroke keys is identical to that for mastering the still frames. First, establish the position physically, referring to the checkpoints that accompany the image. Next, close your eyes and create an image of the position in your mind's eye, giving it as much detail as possible. Notice how the position feels physically, and make the image and the feeling correspond in your mind. Then test the key in controlled drill. As the ball approaches, hold the image of the key in your mind, and as you swing, make your racket, hitting arm, shoulders, etc., overlap the image of the key.

If you visualize the key clearly, it should function as a magnet, attracting your racket and body to the correct position. Hit ten to twenty balls in controlled drill. Rather than using the entire still frame, you may want to visualize just one aspect, such as the wrists at eye level at the Finish Position, the left hitting arm in the double bend position with the wrist laid back at contact, or the tip of the racket pointed straight back at the back fence at the Turn. Experiment with these and other aspects of the images to determine which are best for you.

In addition to these basic keys and their variations, two other more advanced keys are included. These are designed to produce more power and topspin, once the basic stroke is solidly established. The first is the use of extra knee bend. The second key is the brushing action of the racket face on the ball. Create these keys in the same fashion as the others, and test them in controlled drill first. Again, it is important that the basic stroke pattern be solid before you attempt to create additional pace and spin.

Finally, you should develop your tendency analysis for your two-handed backhand. For example, if you or your teaching pro discover that your contact is consistently late, you will want to work extensively with the image of the Contact Point as a key. Or, similarly, if you find that you are having difficulty with the preparation of the racket and/or the body position, you should create a key using the image of the Turn.

As you experiment with developing and refining your keys, systematize them into a stroke key chart. The chart, as shown in the last section of the book, has two parts. First it has space for you to identify as many as four keys that are active for your two-handed stroke. Second, it leaves space for tendency analysis. Here, the player lists his typical errors, and with them the counteracting keys he has developed. You can take the chart with you on the court, and refer to it on the game changes as necessary.

As noted in the sections on keying the other groundstrokes, a major problem most players face is maintaining concentration on the execution of their strokes. The stroke key system provides a framework for achieving this. The images of stroke keys provide a method for producing consistently high-quality tennis, because they can flow through the mind at the same speed the game is actually played on the court.

The keys presented here should be used as a guide in developing your own personal system of two-handed backhand keys. Your goal is to determine which keys are active, and which counteract your own particular tendencies. Test these keys, and others that you or your pro may create, in controlled drill, rallies, and in match play. Compile your chart from the results of this work, and update it frequently.

Keying the Two-Handed Backhand: The Finish Position from the Player's Perspective

○ ○ ○ ○ ○ ○ ○ ○ ○ ○ ○ ○ ○ ○ ○ ○

The Finish Position for the two-handed backhand is the most basic, and usually the most effective, key. If you produce a correct finish, the rest of the stroke leading up to the finish must be correct as well. If you visualize yourself in your mind's eye, you probably will see yourself from over your left shoulder. This is the visual perspective of the key as shown. Note the checkpoints: the left wrist is at eye level, the arm is still in the double bend position, and the racket is straight up and down. The front edge of the racket is perpendicular to the net, and the rear edge is perpendicular to the right shoulder. Establish the position physically and create the mental image. Test the key in controlled drill.

Keying the Two-Handed Backhand: The Turn Position from the Player's Perspective

○ ○ ○ ○ ○ ○ ○ ○ ○ ○ ○ ○ ○ ○ ○ ○ ○

Unless the Turn is correct on the two-handed backhand, as with any groundstroke, it will be impossible to execute a solid stroke. If you are having problems with your preparation, you should work intensively with this key. Again this key is shown from the player's perspective. Note the checkpoints: hitting arm in double bend position, with left elbow into the waist, tip of the racket pointing toward the back fence, face of the racket perpendicular to the court. The racket is also well below waist level. Establish the position physically and create the mental image. Test the key in controlled drill.

Keying the
Two-Handed Backhand:
The Contact Point
from the Player's
Perspective

○ ○ ○ ○ ○ ○ ○ ○ ○ ○ ○ ○ ○ ○ ○ ○

This image is designed to help you create early contact on the two-handed backhand. Usually, a correct finish will ensure that the contact is correct as well. Many players, however, find that using the image of the contact itself is more active. If you find that you are taking the ball late, this key will solve the problem. In addition, players who want to increase their body leverage, and hence the pace of their shot, will find that taking the ball slightly farther in front will produce this result effortlessly.

This key clearly demonstrates the following elements: the shaft of the racket is horizontal, and the face of the racket is perpendicular to the court. The back left shoulder is rotating forward, driving the stroke, with the left, hitting arm in the double bend position. The weight is forward on the front foot, and the Contact well in front of the leg. Establish the position physically and create the mental image. Test the key in controlled drill.

Keying the
Two-Handed Backhand:
Using the Legs
for More Power and Topspin

○ ○

AT THE STEP TO BALL, MAXIMIZE THE KNEE BEND AND THE WEIGHT TRANSFER TO INCREASE SHOT VELOCITY AND TOPSPIN.

One characteristic of all great two-handed players is their use of the legs in the execution of the stroke. Jimmy Connors, Chris Evert, Bjorn Borg, Mats Wilander, and recently Andre Agassi, all generate the pace of their backhand drives in great part from the legs up. By maximizing your knee bend, you guarantee that your legs will release into the shot. As the legs uncoil, they generate additional racket head speed and body leverage. This translates into power, and also, increased topspin. The use of the legs can be the difference between having a solid, consistent two-handed shot, and having the extra velocity that transforms the stroke into a weapon. As you step to the ball, shift your weight fully forward to the front foot, and go down in your knees as far as possible. Establish the position physically, and create the mental image. Test the key in controlled drill.

Keying the
Two-Handed Backhand:
Hitting Up on the Ball
for Topspin

○ ○ ○ ○ ○ ○ ○ ○ ○ ○ ○ ○ ○ ○ ○ ○ ○ ○ ○ ○

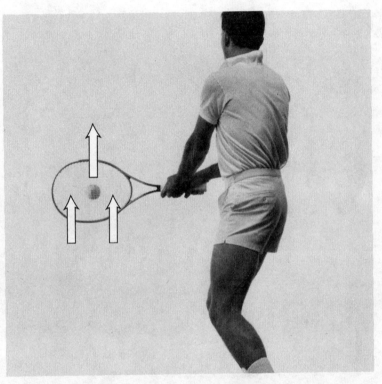

At Contact, THE RACKET FACE MUST BE VERTICAL AND
MOVING SHARPLY UPWARD TO GENERATE ADDITIONAL TOPSPIN.

If you hit the ball with the correct two-handed swing pattern, you should produce topspin automatically. With the racket face vertical at the contact, and accelerating upward, the strings will automatically brush up the backside of the ball and cause it to rotate over itself. As you progress as a player and hit with more pace against better opponents, you may find you need additional spin to keep the ball in the court. Topspin, by causing the ball to travel in an arc, generates additional net clearance, but also causes the ball to drop more sharply, so that it can be hit with more pace and depth without going long. Establish the key physically, and then create the mental image. Visualize the racket moving sharply upward, with the face still vertical, as shown by the arrows. Test the key in controlled drill.

107

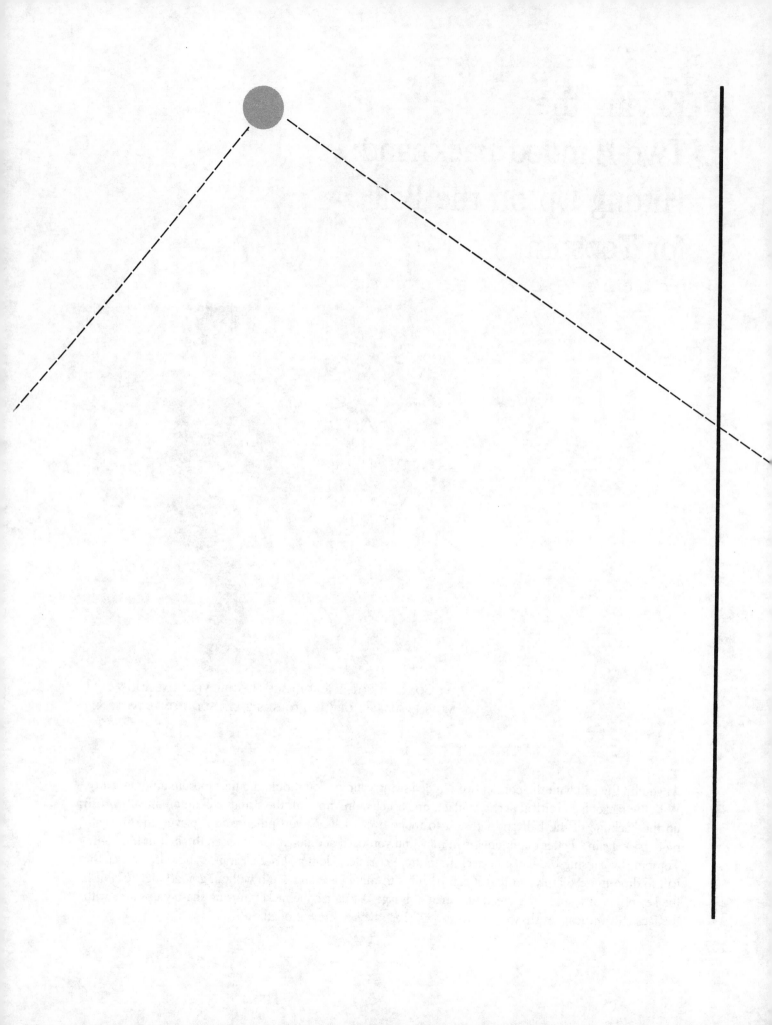

THE RELATIONSHIP BETWEEN TIMING AND POWER

As noted in the chapters on the groundstrokes, one characteristic of great classical players is their smoothness and effortless power. If you watch video of the great players, especially in slow motion, you will note that the racket flows evenly through the stroke. There is no increase in muscle tension as the racket head approaches the contact, no discrete moment when the player "strikes" ball. In fact, there is no perceptible difference between the contact point and every other point on the swing. Possibly the biggest misconception about power on the part of the average player is that hitting the ball harder takes more muscle.

Power, instead, comes from continuous racket head acceleration, and from body leverage. Body leverage is created, as explained in the stroke chapters, by shoulder rotation, by the uncoiling of the legs, and by making contact in front of the body. When the contact is in front of the body as demonstrated in the models, a player ensures that the full leverage generated by the motion will be transferred into the shot.

Therefore, as you develop your stroke patterns for your groundstrokes, you should strive to keep the rhythm of your motion even. This means, whether in controlled drill, rallies, or match play, you should let the ball set the pace. Rather than trying to increase ball velocity by swinging faster, you should imagine yourself hitting the ball back at the speed it is coming. If your technical execution is correct, you will naturally generate pace through the body leverage from the shoulders and legs.

There is a final factor that influences the power of the shot. This is the *timing* of the hit. Taking the ball on the rise, a player can generate extra velocity, without making any change in the stroke pattern itself. This is possible because by taking the ball on the rise, the shot gains velocity from the acceleration of the ball as it comes up off the court. When a tennis ball bounces, the force of hitting the court compresses the ball, partially flattening it out against the court surface. As the ball rebounds and expands back to its original size, it accelerates upward off the court, and its velocity increases. As it approaches the top of the bounce, however, it quickly starts to slow down. This deceleration continues as it reaches the top and starts to drop down. By hitting the ball on the rise, the player catches the ball when it is still accelerating, and therefore this additional velocity is automatically transferred into the shot.

It is important to distinguish here between two terms that are frequently confused. These are hitting the ball "early" and hitting the ball "in front." They are not identical and, in fact, refer to two different aspects of ball contact. Hitting the ball early refers to where the player contacts the ball in relation to the court. The "earlier" the contact, the closer the ball is to the court—the less distance it has traveled toward the top of the bounce.

Hitting in front, on the other hand, refers to where the player contacts the ball *in relation to his body*. Making contact in front, at least with classical stroke patterns, means that the contact point is in front of the edge of the body, usually with the front foot set, so that the full body leverage, from the shoulders and the legs, will be transferred into the shot. It is possible, therefore, to hit the ball in front without hitting it early. For example, the player could let the ball drop below the top of the bounce, and still position himself to strike it with a contact point in front of his body. Conversely, it is also possible to take the ball early, or on the rise, without making contact in front of the body. This is particularly true of the continental strokes. Since it is possible to hit the continental forehand equally well off the back foot, a continental player may actually make contact when the ball is already past the front edge of his body. However, he will still position himself in order to hit the ball *early*. The ball may be behind

his front foot, but he will still strike it on the rise, while it is close to the court, before it reaches the top of the bounce. Actually this is a requirement, since it is almost impossible to execute a solid continental stroke on a high ball.

As demonstrated in the groundstroke chapters, contact in front of the body is a common characteristic of all classical strokes. However, not every classical player takes the ball early. Players such as Chris Evert and Ivan Lendl usually hit the ball at the top of the bounce, or slightly on the way down. One of the great advantages of the classical style is that it allows flexible timing. Indeed, Evert and Lendl often take the ball early when the situation in a given match requires that they do. A classical player has the option to hit the ball at the top of the bounce, on the way down, or to hit it earlier, on the rise.

Early timing, or the ability to hit the ball on the rise, is a characteristic of many of the great champions in the modern game. Jimmy Connors, John McEnroe, Martina Navratilova, and Andre Agassi are players who generate power from taking the ball earlier than other players. In addition to the extra shot velocity, there is a second major advantage to early timing. By taking the ball as it comes up on the court, a player reduces the amount of time his opponent has to recover and prepare for the next shot. Not only does the opponent have to deal with a more powerful shot, he is forced to do it more quickly. If you have ever been on the court with a player of this type of timing, you are aware of the kinds of problems it can cause. The ball comes with laser-like velocity, and is on top of you, or past you, almost before you can react to it. Worst of all, the player who hits the ball early hardly looks like he is working— he is generating the extra pace simply by altering his timing, not by putting more effort into his stroke, and certainly not by using more muscle.

For players developing classical strokes, timing is a final variable with which to experiment. Rather than trying to hit the ball harder by swinging harder and muscling the ball, the classical player who wants additional power should instead experiment with hitting the ball earlier. I have found that some players, even beginners, or intermediate players with relatively poor strokes, will naturally tend to pick the ball up on the rise, without even being told to try this. Similarly, many accomplished players will consistently play the ball after the top of the bounce, and are not comfortable playing the ball early.

As with so many aspects of the game, every player must discover the exact timing that is best for his game. However, the further you progress in the game, and the higher the level of competition, the more important and valuable this ability to hit on the rise becomes. If you find that you would like more pace in your natural stroke patterns, or if you find that you are being consistently outhit by more powerful opponents, you should experiment with your timing.

As with the development of your basic strokes, start by working in controlled drill. Simply step up slightly closer to the oncoming ball, and pick it up before it gets to the top of the bounce. Keep the contact point in front and catch the ball as it is coming up off the court. You may be surprised at the marked increase in the velocity of your shot. You may also find that, initially, this velocity is more difficult to control, and that you hit more balls than usual either long or into the net. Make sure that you keep the swing smooth and relaxed, and that you follow through all the way to the finish position. You may find you need to hit up on the ball slightly more at contact to generate additional topspin to control the extra pace. Also, on the underspin backhand, you may have to hit through the ball slightly more sharply to generate more slice.

Test your early timing in controlled drill with balls hit directly to you, then add movement. If you can produce consistent strokes, progress to rallies, and finally, to matches. If you find that you have a natural affinity for early timing, you can make it a basic aspect of all your groundstrokes. Another option is to hit the ball on the rise only when you are forced to do so by your opponent.

There is no doubt that the degree of difficulty of timing every ball on the rise is much higher than letting the ball drop slightly before contact. That is why you see relatively few players who can do it consistently below the highest levels of the game. Even among the pros, many players do so only when necessity requires. One thing is certain, however: hitting the ball early is the key to producing more power, beyond the execution of a superior technical stroke pattern. If you are continually frustrated by your inability to hit with more power, this is the variable you should strive to master, rather than altering your stroke patterns, overhitting the ball, and producing needless unforced errors.

THE VOLLEY

*I*n one way, the volley is the simplest of all the basic strokes because it has the shortest swing pattern. A good technical volley has no real backswing and very little followthrough. But in another way, the volley is the most difficult. This is because when a player is at the net he is only about half as far away from his opponent, and therefore has only half the time to react and execute the stroke. Although the volley has the least complex motion, it is usually the hardest to hit successfully in matches because the player has such a brief interval.

Playing effective serve and volley tennis is the most dominating, quickest, and possibly most satisfying way to win matches. However, pure serve and volley players are probably born, rather than made. The degree of difficulty of playing serve and volley tennis is much higher than playing in the backcourt, or even playing the all-court game. In the pro game, only two great champions in the last decade, John McEnroe and Martina Navratilova, have been pure attacking players.

Few recreational players can make serve and volley their sole match strategy. But every player can learn to volley confidently using the visualization approach, and, therefore, can learn to incorporate net play into his overall strategy. This means learning to play the all-court game: coming in on short balls when appropriate, and mixing in serve and volley points against certain opponents.

The best definition I have ever heard of the volley is that it is like setting up a mirror in front of a laser beam. The goal is to redirect the laser beam in order to make a superior ball placement. It is rarely necessary to change pace or add speed to an oncoming ball to hit a winning volley. At the net, because you are half as far away from your opponent, the angles between the two players are much sharper. A ball volleyed to the sideline from the net will force a player on the baseline much wider out of the court than a groundstroke hit to the same spot. The more radical angles that are possible at the net are the key to winning placements. To hit a winning volley a player simply redirects his opponent's shots to take advantage of the superior geometry of his position.

Many players are terrified of the net because the play is so much faster there. This fear causes poor shot execution. But this situation, though fairly common, is neither necessary nor inevitable. Any player can learn to volley competently and aggressively if he approaches it correctly.

The first factor that goes into developing the volley is recognizing the crucial role of ball focus. Watching the ball as the opponent makes his shot is a prerequisite for sound volley technique. As you learn the volley in the following sections, it is crucial that you learn to react to the ball as soon as it is hit.

This is only the first step. As stated, the volley requires much less motion than a groundstroke or a serve. But the volley also differs from the other basic shots in another crucial aspect— the earlier contact point. The volley is a reaction or response shot that uses the pace of the oncoming ball. Pace on the volley comes from timing and superior body leverage. To hit the volley with the maximum velocity, therefore, the contact must be significantly further in front of the body than on the groundstrokes. This is the element the majority of recreational players fail to establish. At best, they take the ball at the front edge of the body, as they would a groundstroke. Or worse, they take a large backswing, and make contact behind the plane of the shoulders, attempting to compensate for their lack of technique by overswinging.

In fact, the foreswing on the volley *starts* at about the point where the racket is *contacting* the ball on a good groundstroke. As the racket moves forward, the correct contact point is at least a foot further in front than a groundstroke. In professional tennis, the most aggressive and effective volleyers, players such as McEnroe and Navratilova, are also the players that make the volley look easy. This is due to their timing. By taking the ball further in front than other players, these great champions create superior body leverage. This body leverage means natural power with minimal effort, making the shot look effortless. Taking the ball early at the net is the difference between a good placement that the opponent is able to reach and play back—possibly hitting a passing shot—and a winning volley the opponent has no chance to return. Unless a player understands these differences he will never develop a consistent, effective volley.

Turning to the stroke patterns themselves, there are two major areas of dispute in the theory of the volley which must be addressed. The first is: should the player change grips at the net? The second is: should two-handed backhanders volley with one hand or two?

In my view, there is no absolute answer to the first question of whether to change grips. Jack Kramer virtually invented the serve and volley game, and he changed grips. But Rod Laver and John McEnroe, the two most devastating attacking players to follow Kramer, hit all their volleys with the same continental grip. Martina Navratilova uses the single grip as well. With the increased shot velocity in the modern era, it is probably preferable, at the pro level, to hit all volleys without grip changes.

But for most beginners, and even for some experienced players, this technique will prove much more difficult to master. Therefore, the basic volley models presented here are demonstrated with the same eastern grips as the groundstrokes. There is an additional reason for this. When first learning the volley motions, a player should learn to hit his volleys flat, without underspin, focusing on the bio-mechanics and establishing solid contact. This will happen naturally using the eastern grips.

Once the basic mechanics of the volley

are solid, however, players should experiment with the continental grip. In addition to eliminating the extra time and movement required for the grip shift, the use of the single volley grip makes it easier to hit the ball with underspin, particularly on the forehand side. Underspin gives the player more control of the ball, and is a necessity on low volleys, angled placements, and touch volleys. With the eastern forehand grip it is necessary to use the wrist to dip the racket face sharply under the ball to produce underspin. With the continental grip, however, the player can produce underspin on the forehand while still hitting through the ball on the line of the shot. The change of grip alters the angle of the racket face so that it slides under the ball automatically. The same is true to a lesser extent on the backhand volley, which also requires a slight dipping motion in the swing when hit with the eastern backhand grip, though less so than on the eastern forehand volley.

Since it is more natural to hit the underspin volleys with the continental grip, this is the grip used for the underspin variations presented here. Some players will take to the slice volley with the continental grip quite rapidly. Others, sometimes even players at higher competitive levels, are never able to hit the shot naturally, and are better off sticking with the grip switch at the net. But all players, particularly those with a preference for the attacking style, should at least test the continental grip to see if it will work better for them.

Just as was the case with the groundstroke models, I have chosen to demonstrate the one-handed volley with a straight backswing. If you watch top players, you will see that on the volley, as with the groundstrokes, they initially bend the elbow and raise the racket head as they turn to the ball. Again, this may be a source of additional rhythm and racket head speed. But for the player just trying to develop the shot, it is likely to cause insurmountable difficulties. Top players who use this mini-loop on the volley all keep the *upper* arm (from the elbow to the shoulder) even with the front edge of the shoulders. The racket head then comes forward, in line with the upper arm, and the elbow straightens out somewhat so that the contact point is well in front of the body. Beginning volleyers who try to copy this motion, tend, however, to take the *entire* arm back beyond the plane of the body, ending up with a backswing that is closer to that for a groundstroke and far too large for a volley. This, in turn, produces late contact, the single most common technical error at the net.

It is important initially to develop the feeling of solid, early ball contact on the volley. This is accomplished most easily following the models as shown. After the correct contact point is established, most players will begin to add a little more backswing *naturally*, but this will supplement rather than undermine the fundamentals of the stroke. Trying to create a loop backswing from the beginning will reverse this effect.

As for the second major issue in the theory of the volley, the one-handed versus the two-handed debate, I believe that most two-handed groundstrokers should also learn the two-handed volley. As noted in the chapter on technical styles, it is possible to volley very well with two hands. More relevant, however, is the fact that for most two-handers, it is usually extremely difficult to learn to volley *at all* with one hand. As is the case with the groundstrokes, the bio-mechanics of the one-handed and two-handed backhand volleys are diametrically opposed. A player with no experience hitting with one hand on his groundstrokes starts learning the volley with virtually no muscle memory if he tries to learn with one hand. Making the task even more difficult, he will have to change grips for the first time in his life, and remember to do this at the net regularly, without the habit of doing it in the backcourt. On the other hand, if he has mastered the bio-mechanics of hitting a backhand groundstroke with two hands, he can quickly and naturally draw on this ability in developing a two-handed volley. He will already have developed the basic skill of hitting with the left arm and back left shoulder. The two-handed volley can then be developed as quickly as the two-handed groundstroke, and will produce excellent results mixed in an all-court singles game, and also in doubles.

As also noted in the chapter on the classical style, two-handed players tend to play primarily from the backcourt, and players who want to play attacking tennis should probably develop *both* their backhand groundstrokes and volleys with one hand. For the vast majority of players, continuity on the backhand between their bio-mechanics in the backcourt and at the net will be the best approach.

The volleys presented here are extremely compact technical models. They are based on shoulder turns, and early contact, with virtually no backswing and very little followthrough. The role of the shoulders in the volley has been generally misunderstood in instructional theory. Often the volley is described as a punching motion, implying that the arm extends outward, moving independently of the shoulders and upper body. However, if you observe the top volleyers in the game—John McEnroe, Martina Navratilova, Stefan Edberg, Boris Becker—you will see that the genesis of the motion forward to the ball lies in the rotation of the shoulders. In terms of the bio-mechanics, this is one similarity with the groundstrokes. Compared with the groundstrokes, the amount of rotation is significantly reduced, yet it is still a primary power source, and the key to consistent execution at the high speed of match play. As we will see in the models themselves, good technical volleys have almost no independent arm movement. Instead, the racket can be positioned correctly at the turn solely by the rotation of the shoulders. The motion forward to the early contact point described above is then simply the rotation of the shoulders back toward the original position. This compact turning motion reduces the amount of time necessary to execute the volley to a minimum, and it is something that can be achieved in even the fastest exchanges at net. In contrast, the player who begins his volley motion by taking the arm back and away from the body rarely recovers in time to achieve early contact, and appears to be working very hard, or even flailing at the ball, with little or no result. Pay attention to the role of the shoulders as you develop your stroke and you will volley solidly and aggressively with an economy of motion and effort.

CREATING THE FOREHAND VOLLEY SWING PATTERN

To learn to hit the forehand volley, we will use the same progression as with the groundstrokes, starting with the still frame sequence photos. The sequences will serve as the blueprint for your own swing pattern. Through the techniques presented, you will use them to create a precise *physical* and *visual* model of the stroke.

First, the forehand volley is shown from the front view, and the general technical characteristics of the stroke are outlined. On the following pages, the stroke is shown simultaneously from the front and side views and the four key still frames are isolated. These four still frames are:

1. **The Ready Position**
2. **The Turn**
3. **The Contact Point**
4. **The Finish Position**

As with the groundstrokes, you can see that if the motion is correct at each of the still frames, it will have to be correct throughout the whole pattern. This is particularly true on the volleys because the motions are so much more compact that little that can go wrong in between if the still frame positions are right.

In the following section, each of the four still frames is individually demonstrated, with its checkpoints. You will learn how to create the still frames physically, and also to create a mental image of yourself in each position. After you have learned each still frame, you will see how to put them together into the forehand volley stroke pattern. The following section shows how to do muscle memory corrections for the most common errors. Finally, in the last section, you will learn to create a system of stroke keys to hit reliable forehand volleys under the pressure of match play.

1
READY POSITION

2
START OF TURN

3
THE TURN

Characteristics of the Forehand Volley
FRONT VIEW

○ ○

Grip: When learning the forehand volley, you should start with the same grip as on your forehand groundstroke. The forehand grip variations are discussed in the grip chapter. If, however, your groundstroke grip is an extreme version of the modified eastern, you will probably want to start with a less severe grip on the volley. This sequence is demonstrated with the classic eastern grip, clearly visible in Frame 3.

Ready Position: The forehand volley starts with a Ready Position that differs from the ground-strokes in one vital aspect—the position of the racket head. On the groundstrokes, the racket is below waist level, and points directly at the net. On the volley, the racket head is *high*. The top of the racket should be approximately even with the top of the head (Frame 1). This allows it to move to the Turn *directly* on a straight line (Frames 2 and 3), without wasting time or motion.

Compact Motion: Compared with the groundstrokes, the swing pattern on the volley is extremely brief. There is no backswing as such. Instead, the body and the racket are simply turned

118

4
STEP TO BALL

5
CONTACT POINT

6
FINISH POSITION

sideways to the ball. The racket face never goes further back than the front edge of the shoulders (Frame 3). Likewise, there is very little followthrough. The racket never crosses to the opposite side of the body, as on a groundstroke (Frame 6). Instead, it moves forward on the line of the shot for a maximum of one to two feet.

Minimum Use of Wrist: As is the case with the groundstrokes, the forehand volley is hit with little or no wrist. Instead, the arm is in the double bend position at the Ready Position (Frame 1), the Turn (Frame 3), the Contact Point (Frame 5), and at the Finish Position (Frame 6). Note the elbow is tucked in toward the waist, with the wrist slightly laid back.

Role of Shoulders: Properly executed, the forehand volley is hit almost entirely with shoulder rotation, with a minimum of independent arm motion. In the Ready Position, the shoulders start parallel to the net (Frame 1). At the Turn, they have turned sideways about forty-five degrees (Frame 3). This automatically positions the arm and racket correctly. From the Turn, the shoulders rotate forward, pushing the hitting arm and the racket to the Contact Point (Frame 5) and the Finish (Frame 6). This rotation provides natural body leverage.

Early Contact Point: Compared with the groundstrokes, the Contact Point is much earlier on the volley. In fact, the position of the racket at the Turn (Frame 3) is roughly the same as at the *contact* on most groundstrokes. On the volley, however, the racket then moves forward to the ball, meeting it a foot or more in front of the front edge of the body (Frame 5). This, in conjunction with shoulder rotation, maximizes the natural power of the shot. Early contact is the key to executing the forehand volley consistently, and to generating ball velocity, with little muscle effort.

119

Forehand Volley
Four Key Still Frames · SIDE VIEW

○○○○○○○○○○○○○○○○○○○○○○○○○○○○○○○○○○○

STILL FRAME #1   STILL FRAME #2

READY POSITION   START OF TURN   THE TURN

Forehand Volley
Four Key Still Frames · FRONT VIEW

○○○○○○○○○○○○○○○○○○○○

STILL FRAME #1   STILL FRAME #2

READY POSITION   START OF TURN   THE TURN

STEP TO BALL

CONTACT POINT

FINISH POSITION

STEP TO BALL

CONTACT POINT

FINISH POSITION

121

Still Frame 1
The Ready Position

○ ○ ○ ○ ○ ○ ○ ○ ○ ○ ○ ○ ○ ○

Checkpoints:

1. The Shoulders: The shoulders are parallel to the net. The upper body is straight up and down from the waist. The bend is in the knees.

2. The Hitting Arm: The hitting arm is positioned so that the elbow tucks in toward the waist. The hands are slightly above waist level. Wait with the forehand grip.

3. The Racket: The tip of the racket is even with the top of the player's head. This high racket position is a key difference between the Ready Position on the groundstrokes and that on the volley.

4. The Legs: The legs are shoulder width apart, or slightly wider. The knees are flexed, and the weight is slightly forward on the balls of the feet.

Establish the Ready Position physically using the checkpoints, then create the mental image.

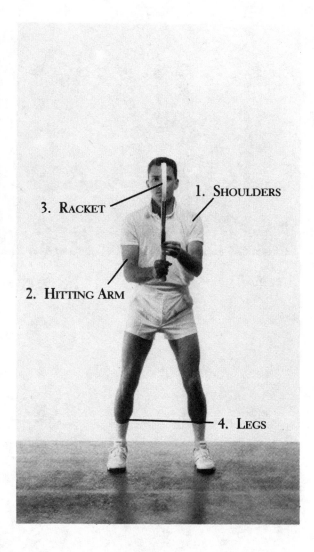

Still Frame 2
The Turn Position

○ ○ ○ ○ ○ ○ ○ ○ ○ ○ ○ ○ ○ ○

Checkpoints:

1. The Shoulders: The shoulders have rotated about forty-five degrees, or half as far as on the groundstrokes. Note that the shoulders, arm, and racket have moved as a unit.

2. The Hitting Arm: The hitting arm remains in the double bend position, with the elbow in and the wrist slightly laid back. It has rotated in position with the shoulder turn.

3. The Racket: The edge of the racket is even with the *front* edge of the shoulders. The shaft of the racket is forty-five degrees to the court surface. The top of the racket is even with the top of the player's head. The *face* of the racket is vertical to the court.

4. The Legs: Both feet have pivoted sideways. The weight is on the right pivot foot, and the left toes are used for balance. The knees are still flexed.

Start in the Ready Position, and move to the Turn. Establish the position physically using the checkpoints, then create the mental image.

3. RACKET

1. SHOULDERS

2. HITTING ARM

4. LEGS

Still Frame 3
The Contact Point

○ ○ ○ ○ ○ ○ ○ ○ ○ ○ ○ ○ ○ ○ ○

Checkpoints:

1. The Shoulders: The shoulders have rotated back toward the net, so that they are almost back to the parallel position, pushing the arm and racket to the contact.

2. The Hitting Arm: There is a slight additional push forward with the hitting arm, following and extending the body rotation. The arm remains in the double bend position, elbow in and wrist back.

3. The Racket: The racket is now about a foot to a foot and a half in front of the body. The shaft is still at a forty-five-degree angle to the court, and the racket face is still vertical.

4. The Legs: The left foot has stepped forward to the ball, with the toes parallel along the edge of a line. The weight is forward on the left front foot. The knees have uncoiled slightly into the ball.

Start in the Ready Position and move through the Turn to the Contact Point. Establish the position physically using the checkpoints, then create the mental image.

Still Frame 4
The Finish Position

○○○○○○○○○○○○○○○○

Checkpoints:

1. **The Shoulders:** The shoulders have continued to rotate slightly further, until they are again parallel with the net. The upper body is still straight up and down from the waist.

2. **The Hitting Arm:** The hitting arm has pushed the racket through the Contact Point, on the line of the shot. The wrist has not released, and the elbow is still slightly bent.

3. **The Racket:** The racket has moved through the ball, with the shaft still at forty-five degrees and with the face of the racket vertical to the court. The butt of the racket now points at the left, opposite hip.

4. **The Legs:** The weight is now fully forward on the left front foot, and the player has come up on his right toes for balance. The knees are still slightly flexed.

Start in the Ready Position, move through the Turn and the Contact Point to the Finish. Establish the position physically using the checkpoints, then create the mental image.

Putting the Still Frames Together
SIDE VIEW

○ ○

READY POSITION   **THE TURN**   **CONTACT POINT**   **FINISH POSITION**

Executing the Forehand Volley

After you have mastered the four key still frames, put them together into a volley swing pattern as shown above. Start in the Ready Position, move to the Turn, forward to the Contact Point, and then to the Finish Position. Make sure that your checkpoints are correct as you pass through each still frame.

Now you are ready to start building your muscle memory. This is a three-step process. First, practice doing correct swings without actually hitting balls, in front of a mirror if possible. Start with one swing, and build up until you can do ten swings and get the checkpoints correct automatically. The goal is to execute the motion correctly without having to think about it.

The second aspect of building muscle memory is hitting balls in controlled drill. Start in the Ready Position at the net. Initially, you should hit volleys that have low to moderate pace, and which come directly to you at about shoulder level. This will allow you to become familiar with the correct execution of the motion and to build up your confidence. As you work in controlled drill, stop every five to ten balls and do muscle memory corrections. The most common corrections are demonstrated in the next section. As with practice swings, work in controlled drill until you can hit ten strokes with little or no correction. Again, set up the controlled drill situation with a practice partner, by working with your teaching pro, or, if possible, by using a ball machine.

When you can hit ten strokes with precision and good technical form, increase the speed of the balls and the number of repetitions. As you start to feel confident, progress to rallies and then to

126

hitting volleys in matches. The last part of the forehand volley chapter shows you how to develop the stroke keys necessary to execute the shot consistently under game pressure.

The third aspect of developing your muscle memory is to practice visualizing the stroke away from the court. This means practicing seeing yourself hitting perfect forehand volleys. As with the other strokes you can do this by sitting down and allocating practice time, or you can do it in free moments in the course of the day when your mind turns to your tennis. Visualize the stroke, and work up to ten visual repetitions. Experiment with visualizing specific keys, as you develop your own key system for the shot.

Finally, you can work visually on your stroke by watching videos of yourself or other players hitting correct forehand volleys. You should do this by watching existing instructional tapes, professional matches, and also by videoing yourself executing perfect practice swings, or hitting the stroke correctly in controlled drill.

Muscle Memory Corrections

○ ○

Compared with the groundstrokes, there is far less followthrough on the volleys. The key aspect is the early contact point. If the contact is correct, then there is a very good likelihood that the shot will be well executed. Because there is far less emphasis on the role of the followthrough in the volley, there is also less emphasis on correcting the followthrough when learning to hit the shot. However, there are some tendencies in execution of the volley that require muscle memory corrections. These are outlined in detail below.

To do a muscle memory correction on the volley, freeze in the statueman position at the end of the shot. Instead of recovering, compare your actual finish with the checkpoints for the correct Finish Position. Then move directly from wherever you are to the correct position. Your muscles will then feel the difference between what they actually did and the right technical motion. This in turn increases the chance that future volleys will follow the model stroke more closely.

The two most common kinds of errors at the finish on the volley are shown below. These are finishing with the racket head in the wrong position, either by releasing the wrist or by hitting down on the ball too sharply, and finishing the shot with incorrect footwork.

If you have either of these two tendencies, doing corrections will eliminate them from your net game. Do the corrections by working in controlled drill. Stop about every five balls and evaluate your finish according to the checkpoints. Now do the correction. As you work, you will find that your corrections become smaller, until your stroke follows the model automatically. In working on your corrections, you should make regular use of video. By watching videos of your actual stroke production, you will not only see how you are deviating from your model, you will develop a clearer image of the model stroke itself.

Muscle Memory Corrections:
Racket Position

These two sequences demonstrate the two most common errors in racket head position at the finish of the volley.

The first error shows the wrist release, which results from overswinging, and trying to hit the ball too hard. The result is actually the opposite of what the player intends. Releasing the wrist destroys body leverage and early contact. It also causes loss of control of the shot placement, the most crucial aspect of aggressive volleying.

The second error is hitting down on the ball too sharply in an effort to produce underspin. The result is late contact, a loss of pace, and a tendency for the ball to float. The correct method for hitting the forehand volley with underspin is demonstrated at the end of this chapter. To correct both these errors, simply freeze in the statueman position. Using the checkpoints for the correct finish, reposition your racket as shown.

STATUEMAN
Wrist Release
and Correction

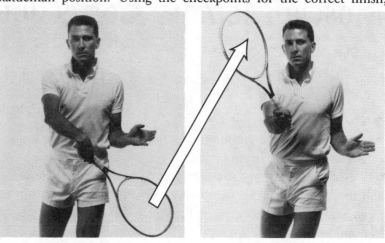

ERROR: WRIST RELEASE   CORRECTED FINISH POSITION

STATUEMAN
Hitting Down (Chop)
and Correction

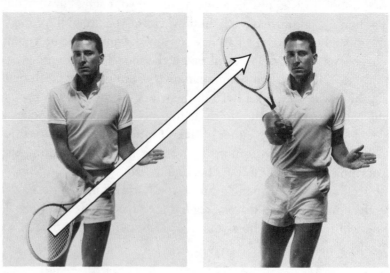

ERROR: HITTING DOWN   CORRECTED FINISH POSITION

128

Muscle Memory Correction:
Leg Position

This sequence shows the most common error in leg position at the finish of the forehand volley: the player has failed to make the step forward to the ball and has finished the volley with an open stance.

Without this step to close the stance, the shot will lack pace. It will be hit late and without any leverage coming from the legs. The amount of shoulder rotation into the ball will be reduced, and the Contact Point will be behind the plane of the body. To correct this error: freeze in the statueman position. Now adjust the feet by stepping across and forward with the left foot so that the toes are parallel along the edge of the line. This will move the weight forward and make the contact early.

STATUEMAN
Open Stance
and Correction

ERROR: OPEN STANCE AT FINISH   **CORRECTED FINISH POSITION**

KEYING THE FOREHAND VOLLEY

After you have worked in controlled drill and have developed your muscle memory, the last step in mastering the forehand volley is developing your system of stroke keys. The keys will give you the ability to hit the shot consistently under match play conditions.

Because of the limited stroke pattern, as noted above, the role of the finish in the volley is reduced compared with the groundstrokes. Instead, the most effective key for the volley is usually the image of the Contact Point. If the Contact Point is correct, the finish will take care of itself on the volley, instead of the other way around. Early contact is the key to handling the pace of the oncoming shot, reflecting that pace into your volley, and making precise ball placements. It is what gives a volley that effortless quality characteristic of the great attacking players.

The first key shown is the image of the Contact Point. Again this is shown from the player's perspective, as you will actually visualize the key in your own mind. You may want to visualize the entire key or focus on one aspect of it—the position of the racket head well in front of the body, the double bend position of the arm, etc.

The second key is the rotation of the shoulders. A common error on the volley is simply to take the arm and racket back independently, without rotating the body. This makes early contact impossible, and decimates the velocity of the shot. If you are not using your shoulders to make the Turn, work with this key.

The third key is the step to the Contact Point. This is a more advanced key. As explained, it allows you to produce the entire stroke simply by keying on the step to the ball, with the shoulders, racket and legs working as a single unit.

The learning procedure for creating your stroke keys is identical to that for mastering the still frames. First, establish the position physically, referring to the checkpoints that accompany the image. Next, close your eyes and create an image of the position in your mind's eye, giving it as much detail as possible. Notice how the position feels physically, and make the image and the feeling correspond in your mind. Then test the key in controlled drill. As the ball approaches, hold the image of the key in mind. As you swing, make your racket, hitting arm, shoulders, and legs overlap the image.

If you visualize the key clearly, it should function as a magnet, attracting your racket and body to the correct position. Hit ten to twenty balls in controlled drill. If the key produces consistent strokes, then it is an active key. Progress to rallies and match play and test the key there. You may also find that

130

slight variations of the key are more effective. For example, rather than using the entire still frame, you may want to visualize just one aspect of the Contact Point, such as the position of the racket head in front of your shoulder, or the double bend position of the hitting arm. Experiment with these and other aspects of the images to determine which are best for you.

The keys presented here should be used as a guide in developing your own personal system of forehand volley keys. Your goal is to determine which keys are active. Compile your stroke key chart from the results of this work, and update it as required. As with the groundstrokes, this should include tendency analysis. Correlate your errors with the counteracting keys, and record them on your chart. You can then take the chart with you on the court, and refer to it during your matches, as needed.

As with the groundstrokes, the keys provide a systematic method for creating and sustaining mental focus under the pressure of match play. Particularly at the net, where everything happens twice as fast, a player's anxieties and fears can dominate his mental processes, making concentration impossible. Because a player can visualize key images even at the high speed of net play, the key system allows a player to stay focused, and to achieve consistent execution on his volleys.

Keying the Forehand Volley: The Contact Point from the Player's Perspective

○ ○

Because the Contact Point is the central aspect of a good technical volley, keying on this image is usually the most effective way to produce the shot in match play. This image is shown from the perspective in which you will probably see yourself in your mind's eye—from slightly over your shoulder and behind. Note the various checkpoints: the shaft of the racket is at about forty-five degrees to the court. The face of the racket is perpendicular. The arm is tucked in toward the waist at the elbow, with the wrist laid back. The right shoulder is rotating forward so that it is solidly behind the shot. Finally, the contact itself is roughly a foot ahead of the body. Establish the position physically and create the mental image. Test the key in controlled drill.

Keying the Forehand Volley: Turn the Shoulders

○ ○

READY POSITION   THE TURN   CONTACT POINT

Shoulder rotation is crucial on the forehand volley. Unless the body rotates, there is a tendency to hit the volley with the arm, to overswing, and to lose power. In the sequence at right, we can see that the shoulders, arm, and racket move as a unit. There is no independent motion. Instead, simply by turning the shoulders, the racket will be positioned correctly. Notice that the hitting arm and racket are already in the double bend position in the first photo of the Ready Position.

This position is maintained in the second photo. The shoulders have rotated forty-five degrees to the net, positioning the racket at the front edge of the body. There is no additional arm movement. In the third photo, the shoulders have now rotated back, pushing the arm and racket to the Contact Point. Thus, the entire stroke can be keyed on the rotation of the shoulders. Establish each of the three positions shown above physically, and create a mental image. The key can be any of the three images, or a mini-movie of the entire shoulder motion. Test the key, or keys, in controlled drill.

Keying the Forehand Volley:
The Cross Step to the Ball

○ ○

READY POSITION **START OF CROSS STEP** **CONTACT POINT**

Once you have mastered the fundamental elements of the forehand volley, it is possible to key the entire stroke on what is called the cross step to the ball. This is often the most effective key for the high speed of match play. Using this key, the shoulders, the racket, and the feet move as a unit to the Contact Point. As shown above, if the step to the ball is correct, the entire motion will be correct as well.

In the Ready Position, imagine that the butt of the racket and the tip of your left toe are attached to each other by a steel rod, shown by the arrows above. In the second frame, you can see that with the racket and foot attached, the shoulders will start to turn and the racket to move forward automatically as the step begins. At the Contact Point, the right shoulder will rotate forward pushing the racket to early contact, as shown in the third frame.

Practice the cross step to the contact, and as you do, create an image of the motion, and of the steel rod connecting your left foot and the butt of the racket. Now test the key in controlled drill.

Variation:
The Underspin Forehand Volley

○ ○

1
READY POSITION

2
START OF TURN

3
THE TURN

Grip: The primary difference in hitting the forehand volley with underspin is the change from the forehand to the continental grip. The grip should be between the eastern forehand and the eastern backhand grip. This means that part of the heel pad of the racket hand is on the top bevel of the frame. The grip chapter demonstrates how to achieve this correctly.

Generating Underspin: The altered grip itself is the only change that is required to add underspin to the shot. By changing to the continental grip, the face of the racket will automatically be slightly open to the surface of the court at the beginning of the motion. This bevel in the racket face angle is clearly visible at the start of the Turn (Frame 2) and at the completion of the Turn (Frame 3). Once the angle of the racket face is set, it remains unchanged throughout the course of stroke. Thus, the face of the racket remains open at the Step to the Ball (Frame 4), at the Contact Point (Frame 5), all the way through to the Finish Position (Frame 6). By moving through the ball at this angle, the strings will automatically slide underneath the ball creating underspin. Imagine the ball as an orange,

4
STEP TO BALL

5
CONTACT POINT

6
FINISH POSITION

and the racket face as a knife. The knife should slice off the diagonal back third of the ball at contact, as with the underspin backhand groundstroke.

Developing the Stroke: Because the bio-mechanics of the underspin volley are similar to the flat volley demonstrated above, there is no need to repeat the progression through the still frames and the checkpoints. If you have developed a solid basic volley, you can add underspin simply by changing the grip and the angle of the racket through the swing. Make sure that you allow the face to open (as it will naturally) at the Start of the Turn (Frame 2). Now complete the motion in the same fashion. Step to the ball, keep the arm in the correct double bend position, and make early contact.

Applications: The underspin volley is necessary for hitting low volleys, and for taking the pace of the ball to make a sharply angled placement or a touch volley. It will also add control on routine volleys at shoulder or waist height. As noted in the Introduction, a major advantage of this shot is that it eliminates the need for grip changes at the net, since the same grip is used for the backhand volley.

Keying the
Underspin Forehand Volley:
Hitting Through the Ball

〇 〇

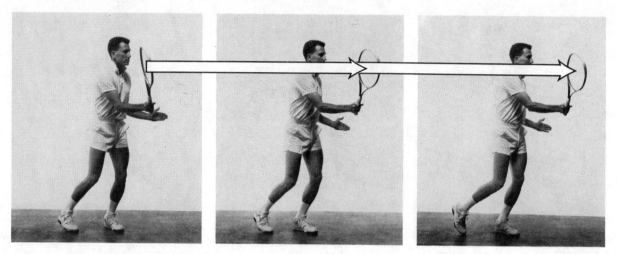

STEP TO BALL   CONTACT POINT   FINISH POSITION

Since the underspin volley shares technical characteristics with the basic, flat forehand volley, most of the keys for the basic shot will apply to the underspin shot as well: these are the image of the early Contact Point, the image of the shoulder turn, and the image of the cross step to the ball.

There is one additional key, however, that is important for the underspin variation. This is the image of hitting through the ball on a straight line. Hitting through the ball is crucial to create body leverage and pace, and for reaching the earliest possible Contact Point. With the racket face open, however, some players will have the tendency to hit down on the ball, believing this is necessary to create spin. The underspin is, in fact, created by the open face moving through the ball. Hitting down will result in late contact and a loss of pace and ball control.

Practice the motion as shown above, moving through the three frames. As you do, create a mental image, or a mini-movie, of the racket face moving through the contact on a straight line. Test the key in controlled drill.

CREATING THE ONE-HANDED BACKHAND VOLLEY SWING PATTERN

In learning the one-handed backhand volley you will follow the familiar visualization progressions, starting with the still frame sequences of the stroke. Using the sequences, you will learn the physical and visual model for the stroke.

The sequences begin by demonstrating the stroke from the front view, and describing the technical characteristics of the shot. The stroke is then shown simultaneously from the front and side, so the four key still frames can be identified. These four frames are:

1. **The Ready Position**
2. **The Turn**
3. **The Contact Point**
4. **The Finish Position**

As is the case with all the strokes, if the motion is correct at these key still frame positions, it will be correct throughout the course of the motion. As with the forehand volley, the backhand volley motion is far more compact than the backhand groundstroke, so there is almost nothing that can go wrong in between if the still frames are correct.

After the still frames are identified, each is individually analyzed and its checkpoints outlined. Using the checkpoints, you will learn how to establish each still frame, and then, to put them together into a smooth stroke. The following sections demonstrate muscle memory corrections and how to create your own system of stroke keys.

1
READY POSITION

2
START OF TURN

3
THE TURN

Characteristics of the One-Handed Backhand Volley FRONT VIEW

○ ○

Ready Position: The Ready Position is the same as for the forehand volley. This means the racket head is up, so that the top of the racket is roughly even with the top of the head (Frame 1). Again this contrasts with the Ready Position for the groundstrokes in which the racket is much lower and points straight at the net.

Grip: The backhand volley is hit with the same grip as the backhand groundstroke. Again, consult the grip chapter if you have a question. In the Ready Position, you should wait with the forehand grip, cradling the throat of your racket with your left hand (Frame 1). The grip change happens as part of the turning motion. This can be clearly seen at the Start of the Turn above (Frame 2). As you start the turn, rotate your right hand toward the top of the frame until you reach your backhand grip position.

138

4
STEP TO BALL

5
CONTACT POINT

6
FINISH POSITION

Compact Motion: As with the forehand volley, the backhand volley is hit with a very compact motion. There is no real backswing with either the arm or racket. Instead, the shoulders are simply turned sideways to the net (Frame 3). This automatically positions the racket at the front edge of the body. From there the racket moves forward only about two feet. The followthrough never crosses to the opposite side of the body, as on a groundstroke (Frame 6).

Minimum Use of Wrist: As with the forehand volley, the backhand volley is hit with minimal or no wrist. At the Turn (Frame 3), the arm and racket are set in the hitting position. The forearm is horizontal to the court, and the wrist is locked. From this position, the arm and racket move forward together as a unit, pushed to the contact by the right front shoulder.

Role of Shoulders: Again, the entire backhand volley can be keyed on the rotation of the shoulders. If the Turn is correct (Frame 3), the right hitting shoulder is positioned at the front edge of the body. The step to the ball (Frame 4) places the weight squarely behind the shot, providing natural body leverage. The shoulder then moves the arm and racket forward to the Contact Point (Frame 5).

Early Contact Point: As with the forehand volley, the Contact Point on the backhand volley is significantly further in front of the body than on the groundstrokes. The position of the racket at the Turn is approximately the same as the Contact Point on the groundstrokes. However, from this point, the racket moves forward to meet the ball. The Contact Point on the volley is an additional one to two feet further in front of the edge of the body (Frame 5). This early Contact Point, combined with the leverage from the shoulders and legs, is the secret to a consistent, effortless backhand volley.

One-Handed Backhand Volley:
Four Key Still Frames · SIDE VIEW

○○○○○○○○○○○○○○○○○○○○○○○○○○○○○○○

STILL FRAME #1   **STILL FRAME #2**

READY POSITION   **START OF TURN**   **THE TURN**

One-Handed Backhand Volley:
Four Key Still Frames · FRONT VIEW

○○○○○○○○○○○○○○○○○○○○○○○○○○○○○○○

STILL FRAME #1   **STILL FRAME #2**

READY POSITION   **START OF TURN**   **THE TURN**

STILL FRAME #3   STILL FRAME #4

STEP TO BALL   CONTACT POINT   FINISH POSITION

STILL FRAME #3   STILL FRAME #4

STEP TO BALL   CONTACT POINT   FINISH POSITION

141

Still Frame 1
The Ready Position

○ ○ ○ ○ ○ ○ ○ ○ ○ ○ ○ ○ ○ ○ ○

Checkpoints:

1. *The Racket:* The tip of the racket is even with the top of the player's head. As with the forehand volley, this higher racket position is a key difference from the Ready Position on the groundstrokes.

2. *The Shoulders:* The shoulders are parallel with the net. The upper body is straight up and down from the waist. The bend is in the knees, not at the waist.

3. *The Hitting Arm:* The hitting arm is positioned so the elbow tucks in slightly toward the waist. The hands are slightly above waist level. Wait with the forehand grip.

4. *The Legs:* The legs are shoulder width apart, or slightly wider. The knees are flexed, and the weight is slightly forward on the balls of the feet.

Establish the Ready Position physically using the checkpoints, then create the mental image.

1. RACKET

2. SHOULDERS

3. HITTING ARM

4. LEGS

Still Frame 2
The Turn Position

○○○○○○○○○○○○○○○

Checkpoints:

1. The Racket: The edge of the racket is even with the front edge of the shoulders. The top of the racket is still even with the top of the player's head. The shaft of the racket is at about a forty-five-degree angle to the court surface. The *face* of the racket is vertical to the court.

2. The Shoulders: The shoulders have rotated about forty-five degrees, or about half as far as on the groundstrokes. The shoulders, hitting arm, and racket have rotated as a unit.

3. The Hitting Arm: The hitting arm has not moved independently, but has swung into position with the shoulder turn. The player has changed to the backhand grip. The forearm is horizontal to the court and the wrist is locked.

4. The Legs: The feet have pivoted sideways. The weight is on the left pivot foot, and the right toes are used for balance. The knees are still flexed.

Move from the Ready Position to the Turn. Establish the position physically using the checkpoints, then create the mental image.

1. RACKET

2. SHOULDERS

3. HITTING ARM

4. LEGS

Still Frame 3
The Contact Point

○ ○ ○ ○ ○ ○ ○ ○ ○ ○ ○ ○ ○ ○ ○

Checkpoints:

1. RACKET
2. SHOULDERS
3. HITTING ARM
4. LEGS

1. *The Racket:* The racket has moved forward to the ball, meeting it at least a foot in front of the edge of the right shoulder. The angle of the racket to the court has not changed. The shaft is about forty-five degrees and the face is still vertical.

2. *The Shoulders:* The shoulders have rotated only slightly. Instead they have stayed basically sideways, keeping the weight behind the ball, while the arm and racket have moved forward.

3. *The Hitting Arm:* The hitting arm has moved forward to the ball as a *unit*. The forearm is still horizontal to the court and the wrist is still locked.

4. *The Legs:* The right foot has stepped forward to the ball, so that the toes are parallel along the edge of a line. The weight is forward on the right foot. The knees have uncoiled slightly into the ball.

Move from the Ready Position through the Turn to the Contact Point. Establish the position physically using the checkpoints, then create the mental image.

Still Frame 4
The Finish Position

○ ○ ○ ○ ○ ○ ○ ○ ○ ○ ○ ○ ○ ○

Checkpoints:

1. RACKET

2. SHOULDERS

3. HITTING ARM

4. LEGS

1. The Racket: The racket has continued straight out through the line of the shot, about a foot past the Contact Point. The shaft is still forty-five degrees to the court, and the face is still vertical. The butt of the racket now points just off the right hip.

2. The Shoulders: The stroke has finished with a minimum of shoulder rotation. The front right shoulder has rotated back just past perpendicular with the net. The upper body is still straight up and down from the waist.

3. The Hitting Arm: There has been no internal movement in the hitting arm through the course of the stroke. The forearm is still horizontal to the court, and the wrist has not released.

4. The Legs: The weight is now fully forward on the right front foot. The player has come up on his rear toes for balance. The knees are still slightly flexed.

Move from the Ready Position through the Turn and the Contact to the Finish Position. Establish the position physically using the checkpoints, then create the mental image.

Putting the Still Frames Together
FRONT VIEW

○ ○

READY POSITION   **THE TURN**   **CONTACT POINT**   **FINISH POSITION**

Executing the One-Handed Backhand Volley

After you have mastered each of the four key still frames, the next step is to put them together into a backhand volley swing pattern as shown above. Start in the Ready Position, now execute the Turn. Step into the ball and move forward to the Contact Point, and then continue to the Finish Position. Make sure that the checkpoints are correct as you pass through each still frame. Again, if you have mastered the still frames and get them correct, this will virtually guarantee that the entire stroke will be correct.

Now build your muscle memory. Again, there is a three-step process. The first step is to practice doing correct practice swings without hitting balls. Start by doing one perfect backhand volley. Build up to ten or more swings. If possible, do this in front of a full-length mirror. The goal is to be able to do the entire motion correctly without having to think about the checkpoints.

The next aspect of building muscle memory is work in controlled drill. Start at the net in the Ready Position. Initially, hit balls that are low to moderate pace and come directly to you at about shoulder height. This will allow you to get comfortable with the basic motion and to build up your confidence. This should be done either using a ball machine, with a practice partner, or with a teaching pro.

As you work in controlled drill, stop every five or ten balls and do muscle memory corrections, as shown in the next section. As with the practice swings, work until you can hit ten strokes with little or no correction.

When you can hit ten strokes with precision and good technical form, increase the speed of the balls, and the number of repetitions. Next, progress to hitting volleys in a rally. Alternate back and forth between the forehand and backhand volley. Be sure to key on the ball as it leaves the opponent's racket so that you start your motion simultaneously with his hit. The last section of this chapter shows you how to develop the stroke keys for the backhand volley, and how to use them to hit the shot under pressure in match play.

The third aspect of developing your muscle memory is to practice simply visualizing the stroke away from the court. You can do this by setting up regular practice time for visualizations, or do it in free moments in the course of your daily routine. Visualize a perfect one-handed backhand volley. Build up to ten visual repetitions. Experiment with visualizing specific keys, as you develop your key system for the shot.

Finally, work on the shot by watching video of good backhand volleys. Do this by watching instructional tapes, taping professional matches and by making a video of yourself executing perfect practice swings and hitting the ball correctly in controlled drill.

Muscle Memory Corrections

As with the forehand volley, the backhand volley has less followthrough than the groundstrokes. Therefore, early contact, rather than the followthrough, is the most important key to good execution. However, there are some tendencies that require muscle memory corrections.

To do a muscle memory correction, freeze in the statueman position at the end of the shot. Do not recover. Instead, hold your position and compare your actual finish with the checkpoints for the correct finish position. Now, move directly to the correct position. Let your muscles feel the difference from what you actually did and what you were trying to do. This will increase the probability that the next shot will follow the model more closely, and over time, will bring the two in line.

The two most common types of errors are outlined below. They are finishing the shot with the racket head in the wrong position and finishing the shot with an open stance. Do the corrections by working in controlled drill. Stop about every five balls and evaluate and correct your finish according to the checkpoints. You will find that your errors become smaller and smaller until your stroke follows the model automatically. In working on your corrections, you should make regular use of video. By watching video of your actual stroke production, you will not only see how you are deviating from your model, you will develop a clearer image of the model stroke itself.

Muscle Memory Corrections:
Racket Position

The two sequences on this page show two common errors in racket head position at the Finish of the backhand volley.

The first is releasing the wrist. This comes from overswinging in an effort to hit the ball too hard. The result is that the player loses the early Contact Point and natural body leverage, creating the opposite effect—instead of more power, there is usually less, as well as a loss of ball control.

The second error is hitting straight down on the ball, rather than *through* the ball on the line of the shot. Usually, players who make this error are trying to generate underspin, but instead, this chopping motion causes the ball to float and lose pace. The correct approach for hitting underspin on the backhand volley is demonstrated in a following section. To correct these errors, freeze in the statueman position. Then use the checkpoints to reposition your racket as shown.

STATUEMAN
Wrist Release
and Correction

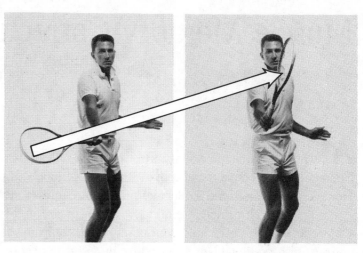

ERROR: WRIST RELEASE   CORRECTED FINISH POSITION

STATUEMAN
Hitting Down (Chop)
and Correction

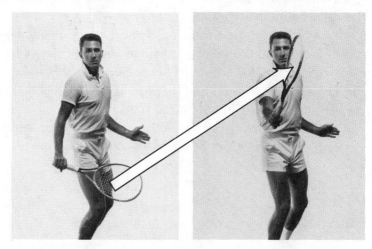

ERROR: HITTING DOWN   CORRECTED FINISH POSITION

Muscle Memory Correction:
Leg Position

This sequence shows the most common error in the footwork on the backhand volley: finishing with an open stance.

The player has failed to step parallel to the ball, as shown in the first photo below. Without this step, the shoulder turn will never be complete, and the body weight cannot be transferred into the shot through the front leg. The result is late contact. The pace of the shot will be reduced, and the swing will tend to be too sharply down instead of out through the ball.

To correct this error, freeze in the statueman position. Now adjust the feet to the correct position by stepping across and forward with the right foot. The toes of the feet should be parallel along the edge of a straight line. The result will be the creation of body leverage, and an early contact.

STATUEMAN
Open Stance
and Correction

ERROR: OPEN STANCE AT FINISH   CORRECTED FINISH POSITION

KEYING THE ONE-HANDED BACKHAND VOLLEY

As with the forehand volley, the next step after developing your muscle memory is creating a personal system of stroke keys. The keys are images of basic elements of the stroke. By visualizing them, you activate the entire stroke pattern, and are then able to execute the shot under the pressure of match play.

Because of the reduced role of the followthrough compared with the groundstrokes, the most important key on the backhand volley is usually the image of the Contact Point. Early contact allows you to use the pace of the oncoming ball to create your own power, and to develop precise ball control. Therefore, the image of the Contact Point, and how to use it, is the first key demonstrated in this section.

The second key is the rotation of the shoulders. If a player can achieve the correct shoulder turn on the one-handed backhand volley, he will position the arm and racket automatically, with no additional motion. Many players make the mistake of taking the arm and racket back independently of the shoulders, virtually guaranteeing late ball contact and a loss of power. Often they overcompensate for a poor turn by overswinging, further increasing the chance of error. This key is designed to help you establish the turn, and develop solid contact using body leverage, not the swing, for power.

The third key in this section is the step to the ball. This is an advanced key which allows the player to generate the entire shot by keying on the cross step. As demonstrated, it allows the legs, racket and body to work as a unit. It is the most effective key for many players given the reduced time available to execute a shot at net.

The learning procedure for creating your stroke keys is identical to that for mastering the still frames. First, establish the position physically, referring to the checkpoints that accompany the image. Next, close your eyes and create an image of the position in your mind's eye, giving it as much detail as possible. Notice how the position feels physically, and make the image and the feeling correspond in your mind. Then test the key in controlled drill. As the ball approaches, hold the image of the key in mind. As you swing, make your racket, hitting arm, shoulders, and legs overlap the image.

If you visualize the key clearly, it should function as a magnet, attracting your racket and body to the correct position. Hit ten to twenty balls in controlled drill. If the key produces consistent strokes, then it is an active key. Progress to rallies and match play and test the key there. You may also find that slight variations of the key are more effective. For example, rather than using the entire still frame, you may want to visualize just one aspect of the image. Experiment with these and other aspects of the images to determine which are best for you.

The keys presented here should be used as a guide in developing your own personal system of backhand volley keys. Your goal is to determine which keys are active, and which counteract your own particular tendencies. Correlate your errors with the counteracting keys. Test the keys, and others that you may discover, in controlled drill, rallies, and in match play. Compile your stroke key chart from the results of this work, and update it as required. As with the forehand volley, your stroke key chart provides a reliable method for creating mental focus in match play and avoiding panic at the net, even in the face of the rapid-fire exchanges that are a regular part of net play. By using it, you will develop the ability to execute backhand volleys with routine precision and success.

Keying the One-Handed Backhand Volley: The Contact Point from the Player's Perspective

○ ○ ○ ○ ○ ○ ○ ○ ○ ○ ○ ○ ○ ○ ○ ○ ○ ○ ○ ○

As with the forehand volley, the most effective key for the backhand volley is usually the image of the Contact Point. If the contact is early, the shot will have body leverage and natural pace. You will control the placement of the ball, and the stroke will feel effortless.

This image is shown from the perspective you will probably see yourself from in your mind's eye. Note the checkpoints. The shaft of the racket is about forty-five degrees to the court. The face of the racket is perpendicular. The forearm is horizontal, with the elbow slightly bent, and the wrist is locked. Finally, the contact with the ball is at least a foot in front of the right shoulder. Establish the position physically and create the mental image. Test the key in controlled drill.

Keying the One-Handed Backhand Volley: Turning from the Shoulders

○ ○

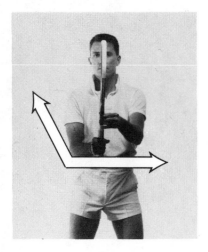  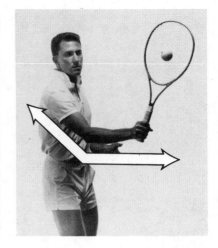

A common error on the backhand volley is to backswing with the arm and the racket, taking them back without turning. As this sequence shows, the arm and racket stay in virtually the same position throughout the motion.

In the Ready Position, the elbow is in toward the waist, and the forearm is horizontal, or parallel, to the court surface. To make the Turn, the player has rotated his shoulders sideways. The arm and racket will then move as a unit. The elbow is still bent and points in, and the forearm has remained horizontal.

At the Contact Point, this relationship is preserved. The hitting arm and racket have swung forward like a gate on the hinge of the shoulder, with the elbow bent and the forearm still parallel to the court. There are no independent moving parts.

Go through the motion shown above moving the shoulders, hitting the arm, and racket. Create a mental image, or mini-movie, of the motion. Test the key in controlled drill.

Keying the One-Handed Backhand Volley: The Cross Step to the Ball

READY POSITION   START OF CROSS STEP   CONTACT POINT

Once you have mastered the elements of the one-handed backhand volley, you can key the stroke on the cross step to the ball. This is usually an effective key at the high speed of match play, but it also requires that you build up strong muscle memory in controlled drill, so that when you make the cross step, the other elements of the motion remain correct. This allows you to execute the backhand volley with one quick step in match play.

In the Ready Position, imagine that the butt of the racket and the tip of your right toe are attached to each other by a steel rod, shown by the arrows above. In the second frame, you can see that with the racket and foot attached, the shoulders will start to turn and the racket to move forward automatically as the step begins. At the Contact Point, the right shoulder pushes the hitting arm and racket to meet the ball early and in front of the body, as shown in the third frame. Practice the cross step to the contact, and as you do create a mental image of the motion.

Variation:
The Underspin Backhand Volley

○ ○

1
READY POSITION

2
START OF TURN

3
THE TURN

Grip: For the underspin backhand volley use the same continental grip as for the underspin forehand volley. Most players find it easier to produce underspin with this grip than with the more extreme eastern backhand, because it is possible to hit through the line of the shot more easily. This will allow you to hit both volleys with the same grip, and eliminate the grip shift at the net, a major advantage in playing attacking tennis.

Generating Underspin: To create underspin, the key is to set the angle of the racket face correctly at the Start of the Turn (Frame 2). You can see in this frame that the racket face is already slightly open. This is accomplished by rotating the wrist and forearm slightly backward as the motion starts. By the time the Turn is complete (Frame 3), the face of the racket is beveled so that it is at about a thirty-degree angle with the court. Once the angle of the racket face is set, it remains *unchanged* throughout the remaining course of the motion. Thus the racket face remains slightly open at the Step to Ball (Frame 4), at the Contact Point (Frame 5), and at the Finish Position (Frame 6). It has moved straight through the motion on the line of the shot, rather than downward. The angle of the racket face slides under the ball creating underspin automatically, just as on a slice backhand groundstroke.

4
STEP TO BALL

5
CONTACT POINT

6
FINISH POSITION

Developing the Stroke: The basic bio-mechanics of the underspin volley are identical to the flat volley demonstrated earlier, with the exceptions of the change of grip and racket face angle. Therefore, there is no need here to repeat the progression through the still frames and the checkpoints. If you have developed a solid flat volley, you can add the underspin by simply altering the angle of the racket face at the start of the Turn. This is true no matter which volley grip you adopt. The other key elements are the same. The Turn is generated from the shoulders. There is no backswing. The hitting arm and racket stay in the same position throughout the stroke, and the contact is well in front of the right shoulder.

Applications: The underspin backhand volley can be used to make any shot previously made with the flat volley. The underspin gives the player more control of the speed and placement. It is also a necessity for low volleys, sharply angled, or touch volleys. Therefore, with underspin, the player hits all backhand volleys with the same basic bio-mechanics.

Keying the Underspin Backhand Volley: Hitting Through the Ball

○ ○

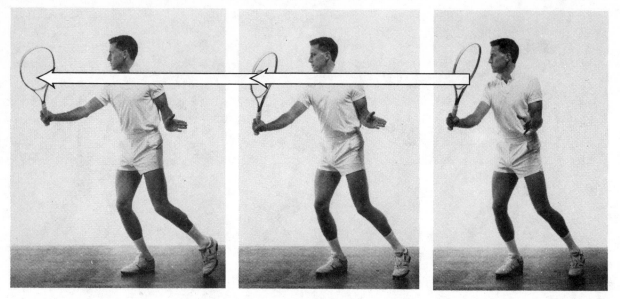

FINISH POSITION   CONTACT POINT   STEP TO BALL

Because it shares the basic technical characteristics of the flat volley, most of the same keys will apply equally well to the underspin variation. These include the image of the early Contact Point, the image of the shoulder turn, and the cross step to the ball.

As with the underspin forehand volley, however, there is one additional key that is important to solid execution. This is the image of hitting through the ball on a line. Because the racket face is open at the turn on the underspin volley, some players will tend to hit *down* rather than *through*. The result is late contact, a loss of body leverage, and, therefore, poor ball control and reduced pace. In reality it is the angle of the racket face that creates the spin, not the downward angle of the swing plane.

Practice the motion as shown above, moving through the three frames. As you do, create a mental image, or a mini-movie, of the open racket face moving through the contact on a straight line. Test the key in controlled drill.

156

CREATING THE TWO-HANDED BACKHAND VOLLEY SWING PATTERN

The progression for developing the two-handed backhand volley is based on the same still frame photo sequences as the other volleys. These sequences are used, as with the others, to create a physical and visual model of the swing pattern.

The progression begins by showing the two-handed backhand volley from the front view, and explaining the general technical characteristics of the stroke. Next, the stroke is demonstrated simultaneously from the front and the side, and the four key still frames are identified. The four still frames are:

1. **The Ready Position**
2. **The Turn**
3. **The Contact Point**
4. **The Finish Position**

If the player's two-handed backhand volley is correct at each of these four still frames, it will *have* to be correct throughout the course of the motion. Because the motion is so compact, there is virtually nothing that can go wrong between the still frames if they are each correct.

After the four still frames are identified, each one is individually demonstrated, and the checkpoints are outlined. Using the checkpoints you will learn to physically establish the still frames, how to visualize yourself in each still frame position, and then, how to put the frames together into a smooth overall stroke pattern.

The following two sections demonstrate muscle memory corrections for the two-handed backhand volley and the strokes keys that are the basis for the consistent execution of the shot in match play.

157

1
READY POSITION

2
START OF TURN

3
THE TURN

Characteristics of the
Two-Handed Backhand Volley
FRONT VIEW

Grip: The two-handed backhand volley is hit with *two* forehand grips, just as with the two-handed backhand groundstroke. The right hand forehand grip is maintained, and a second forehand grip is added with the left hand. The two hands are together, touching, but not overlapping on the racket handle, as can be clearly seen in Frame 2. Again, if you play with two hands, you should wait in the Ready Position with the two-handed grip. The racket head is up, with the top of the frame even with the top of the head, as is the case with either the forehand or the one-handed backhand volley.

Similarity to Two-Handed Groundstroke: The bio-mechanics of the two-handed backhand volley are similar to the two-handed groundstroke in one key respect: the *left*, back arm is the hitting arm. The left arm and the left shoulder generate the motion, almost identically to a left-handed forehand volley. The right arm adds additional, but secondary support. In Frames 4 through 6, you can see the *left* shoulder rotating forward, and the left arm pushing the racket forward to the Contact Point.

4
STEP TO BALL

5
CONTACT POINT

6
FINISH POSITION

Minimum Use of Wrist: The position of the left hitting arm on the two-handed volley is the same as the right arm on the forehand volley. This means the arm is in the double bend position, with the elbow in toward the waist, and the wrist slightly laid back. The forearm is horizontal to the court. The arm and wrist are already in the double bend in the Ready Position (Frame 1). This double bend alignment remains unchanged throughout the motion. The hit is generated from the back left shoulder. The wrist does not release at contact (Frame 5) and is still laid back at the Finish Position (Frame 6).

Compact Motion: As with the other volleys, there is no backswing. The shoulders are turned sideways to the net (Frame 3), and this turn automatically positions the racket at the front edge of the body. From this position, the racket moves forward to the contact and the finish, a total of about two feet. The followthrough never crosses to the opposite side of the body. At the end of the stroke, the butt of the racket points just off the right front hip (Frame 6).

Early Contact Point: Again, the Contact Point is earlier than for the groundstrokes. At the completion of the Turn, the racket is at the front edge of the body, which is the approximate Contact Point on the groundstrokes. From this point the racket moves *forward* to the contact about a foot in front of the body (Frame 5). This early timing generates natural body leverage and shot velocity. It is what gives the volley a solid, effortless feel.

159

Two-Handed Backhand Volley:
Four Key Still Frames · FRONT VIEW

○ ○

STILL FRAME #1   STILL FRAME #2

READY POSITION   START OF TURN   THE TURN

Two-Handed Backhand Volley:
Four Key Still Frames · SIDE VIEW

○ ○

STILL FRAME #1   STILL FRAME #2

READY POSITION   START OF TURN   THE TURN

STILL FRAME #3　　　　　　STILL FRAME #4

STEP TO BALL　　　　　　CONTACT POINT　　　　　　FINISH POSITION

STILL FRAME #3　　　　　　STILL FRAME #4

STEP TO BALL　　　　　　CONTACT POINT　　　　　　FINISH POSITION

Still Frame 1
The Ready Position

○ ○ ○ ○ ○ ○ ○ ○ ○ ○ ○ ○ ○ ○ ○

Checkpoints:

1. The Racket: The tip of the racket is even with the top of the head. The hands are together in the two-handed backhand grip. Wait with this grip for both the forehand and backhand volley.

2. The Shoulders: The shoulders are parallel with the net. The upper body is straight up and down from the waist. The bend is at the knees, not the waist.

3. The Hitting Arm: The *left* hitting arm is positioned so that the elbow tucks in toward the waist, with the wrist laid back. The forearms are parallel to the court.

4. The Legs: The legs are shoulder width apart, or slightly wider. The knees are flexed, and the weight is forward on the balls of the feet.

Establish the Ready Position physically using the checkpoints, then create the mental image.

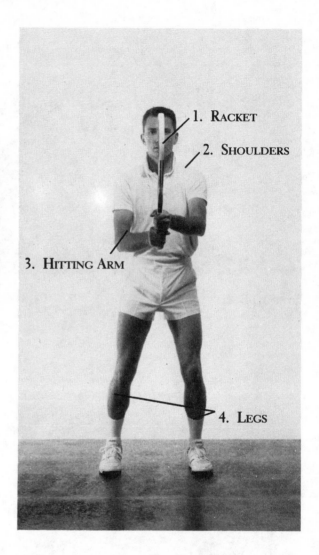

1. RACKET

2. SHOULDERS

3. HITTING ARM

4. LEGS

Still Frame 2
The Turn Position

○ ○ ○ ○ ○ ○ ○ ○ ○ ○ ○ ○ ○ ○ ○

Checkpoints:

1. The Racket: The top of the racket is still even with the top of the head. The *edge* of the racket is even with the front edge of the shoulders. The shaft of the racket is forty-five degrees to the court. The face of the racket is vertical.

2. The Shoulders: The shoulders have turned about forty-five degrees or slightly more. The shoulders, hitting arm, and racket have rotated as a unit.

3. The Hitting Arm: The hitting arm has not moved independently, but has swung into position automatically with the shoulder turn. Both forearms are horizontal to the court. The left wrist is slightly laid back.

4. The Legs: Both feet have pivoted sideways. The weight is on the left pivot foot, and the right toes are used for balance. The knees are still flexed.

Start in the Ready Position and move to the Turn. Establish the position physically, using the checkpoints, then create the mental image.

1. RACKET

2. SHOULDERS

3. HITTING ARM

4. LEGS

Still Frame 3
The Contact Point

○ ○ ○ ○ ○ ○ ○ ○ ○ ○ ○ ○ ○ ○ ○

Checkpoints:

1. RACKET

2. SHOULDERS

3. HITTING ARM

4. LEGS

1. The Racket: The left arm has pushed the racket forward to the ball, with contact at least a foot on front of the body. The shaft is forty-five degrees to the court, and the face of the racket is still vertical.

2. The Shoulders: The left shoulder has generated the hit by rotating forward and around, pushing the left arm and racket forward to the Contact Point.

3. The Hitting Arm: There is a slight additional push forward with the hitting arm to reach the contact. The hitting arm and racket have done this by moving as a unit. The right arm adds only secondary support.

4. The Legs: The right foot has stepped forward to the ball, with the toes parallel along a line. The weight is forward on the front foot. The knees have uncoiled slightly into the ball.

Start in the Ready Position and move through the Turn to the Contact. Establish the position physically using the checkpoints, then create the mental image.

Still Frame 4
The Finish Position

○ ○ ○ ○ ○ ○ ○ ○ ○ ○ ○ ○ ○ ○

Checkpoints:

1. *The Racket:* The racket has moved through the Contact Point to the Finish with the shaft still at forty-five degrees, and the face still vertical to the court. The butt of the racket now points at the right hip.

2. *The Shoulders:* The shoulders have continued to rotate slightly further past the Contact Point, until they are almost parallel to the net. The upper body is still straight up and down at the waist.

3. *The Hitting Arm:* The hitting arm has pushed the racket through the Contact Point to the Finish Position, along the line of the shot. There has been no internal movement of the arm and racket. The elbow is still bent and the wrist laid back.

4. *The Legs:* The weight is now fully forward on the right front foot. The player has come up on his right rear toes for balance. The knees are still slightly flexed.

Move from Ready Position through the Turn and the Contact to the Finish. Establish the position physically using the checkpoints, then create the mental image.

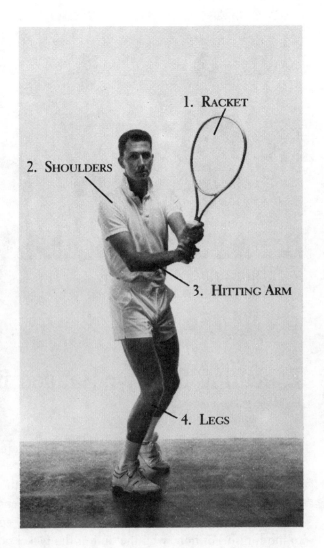

1. RACKET

2. SHOULDERS

3. HITTING ARM

4. LEGS

Putting the Still Frames Together
SIDE VIEW

○ ○

READY POSITION   **THE TURN**   **CONTACT POINT**   **FINISH POSITION**

Executing the Two-Handed Backhand Volley

After you have mastered the still frames individually, the next step is to put them together into the swing pattern, as shown above.

Start in the Ready Position. Pivot on the balls of the feet, turn the shoulders, and move to the Turn. Now step parallel, increase the knee bend, and with the left shoulder and hitting arm, push the racket forward to the Contact Point. Finally, continue the shoulder rotation, and move the racket to the Finish Position, with the butt of the racket pointing at the right hip.

As you pass through the still frames, make sure each of the checkpoints is correct. If you are unsure of any aspect of the motion, stop and verify the individual checkpoints. If the still frames are correct, it will virtually guarantee that the entire pattern will be correct as well.

Now begin the three-step process to develop your muscle memory on the shot. First, practice executing the swing pattern without hitting balls. This can be done at home, in front of a mirror if possible.

Start by executing one perfect two-handed backhand volley. Make sure the checkpoints are correct. Build up to ten or more swings. Your goal is to execute the motion correctly without having to stop and refer to the checkpoints.

The next aspect of building muscle memory is hitting balls in controlled drill. Start at the net in Ready Position. Initially, you should hit balls that are low to moderate in pace, and that come directly to you at about shoulder height. You can create controlled drill using a ball machine, with a practice partner or your teaching pro. This work will allow you to become comfortable executing the shot, and will build up your confidence.

As you work in the controlled drill stop every five to ten balls and do a muscle memory correction, as demonstrated in the next section. As with the practice swings, work until you can hit ten strokes with little or no correction.

When you can execute ten volleys with consistently correct technique, increase the speed of the balls and the number of repetitions. Alternate back and forth between the backhand and the forehand volleys.

Now you are ready to progress to rallies. Be sure to focus on the ball as it leaves the opponent's racket, so that you start your motion simultaneously with the hit. The last section on the two-handed backhand volley will show you how to develop the stroke keys for this shot, and how to use them to execute under pressure in matches.

The final aspect of developing muscle memory is to practice visualizing the stroke away from the court. You can do this by setting aside regular times to practice your visualizations, or by doing them in free moments in the course of your daily routine. Visualize yourself hitting a perfect two-handed backhand volley. Build up to ten repetitions. Experiment with visualizing specific keys, as you develop your key system for the shot. In addition, you should work visually by watching video of the backhand volley. You can use instructional videos, watch tapes of professional matches, and also make a video of yourself executing perfect practice swings and hitting the shot correctly in controlled drill.

Muscle Memory Corrections

○ ○

As with the other volleys there is minimal followthrough in the two-handed backhand volley. However, using muscle memory corrections at the Finish Position is important to eliminate certain common errors.

The three most frequent errors and their corrections are demonstrated below. These are errors in racket position, and in footwork. To make a muscle memory correction, freeze at the end of the shot in the statueman position. Do not recover. Hold this position, and compare your actual finish with the checkpoints for the correct finish. Now move directly from your actual position to the correct one. This process teaches your muscles to feel the difference between what you were trying to do and what you actually did. As with the groundstrokes and other volleys, doing muscle memory corrections over time will bring your stroke closer to the model, until you are executing it correctly on a consistent basis. Again, in working on your corrections, you should make regular use of video. By watching video of your actual stroke production, you will not only see how you are deviating from your model, you will develop a clear image of the model stroke itself.

Muscle Memory Corrections: Racket Position

The next two sequences show two common errors in the racket position at the finish of the two-handed backhand volley.

The first is releasing the wrists at the Contact Point. Doing this, in an attempt to hit with more pace, the player actually cuts off his body leverage, creating a loss instead of a gain. Releasing the wrists also causes sudden changes in the direction of the racket head, which results in a lack of control over shot placement.

The second error is releasing the left hand at contact. This error causes the player to lose the primary source of leverage on the shot, which is the body rotation, and the pushing action of the back, left hitting arm. The result is chronically late contact. The player has a difficult time controlling shots hit to him with pace, and again, he loses ball control.

To correct these errors, simply freeze in the statueman position, then, referring to the checkpoints if necessary, reposition the racket to the correct Finish Position as shown.

STATUEMAN
Wrist Release
and Correction

ERROR: WRIST RELEASE   CORRECTED FINISH POSITION

STATUEMAN
Releasing the Left Hand
and Correction

ERROR: RELEASING LEFT HAND   CORRECTED FINISH POSITION

Muscle Memory Correction:
Leg Position

This sequence shows a typical footwork error on the two-handed backhand volley, finishing with an open stance. The player in the first photo has not stepped forward into the ball. Without this step to the ball, the stance will be open at the Finish Position. The shoulder turn will not be complete, limiting the body rotation. In addition, the body weight cannot be transferred into the shot. As a consequence, the swing pattern will often be too sharply down, the contact will be late, and the shot will tend to float. To correct this error, freeze in the statueman position. Now adjust the feet to the correct position by stepping across and forward with the right foot. The toes of the feet should be parallel along the edge of a straight line.

STATUEMAN
Open Stance
and Correction

ERROR: OPEN STANCE AT FINISH CORRECTED FINISH POSITION

169

KEYING THE TWO-HANDED BACKHAND VOLLEY

As with the other volleys, the final step in learning to execute the two-handed volley in match play is to develop your stroke key system. Again, the most effective key for most players is the image of the early contact. Early contact is the key to effortless power and good ball control. It is the first key outlined below.

The second key is the shoulder rotation. A fatal error made frequently at the net is to take the arm and racket back independently, rather than allowing the shoulder turn to swing them into position. Working with this key, you can correct this problem, and assure the role of body rotation in the stroke.

The third key, as in the case of the other volleys, is the cross step to the ball. A more advanced key, it allows you to produce the entire stroke pattern by keying on a single step to the ball. With this key, the racket, the shoulders, and the legs move as a unit. It allows the player to execute solid technical volleys in the rapid-fire exchanges of net play.

The learning procedure for creating your stroke keys is identical to that for mastering the still frames. First, establish the position physically, referring to the checkpoints that accompany the image. Next, close your eyes and create an image of the position in your mind's eye, giving it as much detail as possible. Notice how the position feels physically, and make the image and the feeling correspond in your mind. Then test the key in controlled drill. As the ball approaches, hold the image of the key in mind. As you swing, make your racket, hitting arm, shoulders, and legs overlap the image.

If you visualize the key clearly, it should function as a magnet, attracting your racket and body to the correct position. Hit ten to twenty balls in controlled drill. If the key produces consistent strokes, then it is an active key. Progress to rallies and match play and test the key there. You may also find that slight variations of the key are more effective. For example, rather than using the entire still frame, you may want to visualize just one aspect of the image.

The keys presented here should be used as a guide in developing your own personal system of two-handed backhand volley keys. Your goal is to determine which keys are active, and which counteract your own particular tendencies. Correlate your errors with the counteracting keys. Test the keys, and others that you may discover, in controlled drill, rallies, and in match play. Compile your stroke key chart from the results of this work, and update it as required. Your stroke key chart provides a reliable method for creating mental focus in match play and avoiding panic in the face of the rapid-fire exchanges at the net. By using it, you will develop the ability to execute two-handed backhand volleys with routine precision and success.

Keying the Two-Handed Backhand Volley: The Contact Point from the Player's Perspective

○ ○

Early contact is the most powerful key on any volley, and the two-handed backhand is no exception. The image here is shown from the player's perspective from over the shoulder and slightly behind.

Note the position of the various checkpoints. The shaft of the racket is about forty-five degrees to the court. The face of the racket is vertical. The elbow of the left, hitting arm is slightly bent, and the wrist is laid back. The left shoulder has rotated forward, pushing the arm and the racket to the ball, and creating natural body leverage. Finally, the contact is about a foot in front of the body. Establish the Contact Point physically and create a mental image. Test the key in controlled drill.

Keying the Two-Handed Backhand Volley: Turning from the Shoulders

○ ○

READY POSITION · THE TURN · CONTACT POINT

172

A crucial aspect of the two-handed volley is the use of shoulder rotation. The arm and racket should never go back independently, but move in unison with the shoulders. As the first image above shows, the shoulders start parallel to the net.

In the second image, the shoulders have turned to the ball, so that they are about forty-five degrees to the net. By making this rotation, the player swings the hitting arm and racket into correct position. In the third image, the shoulders have rotated back toward the parallel position, pushing the hitting arm and racket forward to the ball. The result is early contact and natural power. Move through the motion several times as shown above, keying on the role of the shoulders. As you do, create a mental image, or a mini-movie of the movement. Now test the key in controlled drill.

Keying the Two-Handed Backhand Volley: The Cross Step to the Ball

○ ○

READY POSITION   **START OF CROSS STEP**   **CONTACT POINT**

As with all volleys, the two-handed backhand volley can be keyed on the cross step to the ball. This key allows the player to execute the shot consistently in high-speed exchanges. With the step, as the sequence shows, the shoulders, arm, and racket all move as a unit to the ball. However, the use of this key requires mastery of the other basic elements and should be used only when the muscle memory for the stroke has been firmly established.

In the Ready Position, imagine that the butt of the racket and the tip of your right toe are attached to each other by a steel rod, shown by the arrows above. In the second frame, you can see that with the racket and foot attached, the shoulders will start to turn and the racket to move forward automatically as the step begins. At the Contact Point, the left rear shoulder pushes the hitting arm and racket forward to meet the ball early, as shown in the third frame.

Practice the cross step to the contact, and as you do create a mental image of the motion, and of the steel rod connecting your right foot and the racket butt. Now test the key in controlled drill.

173

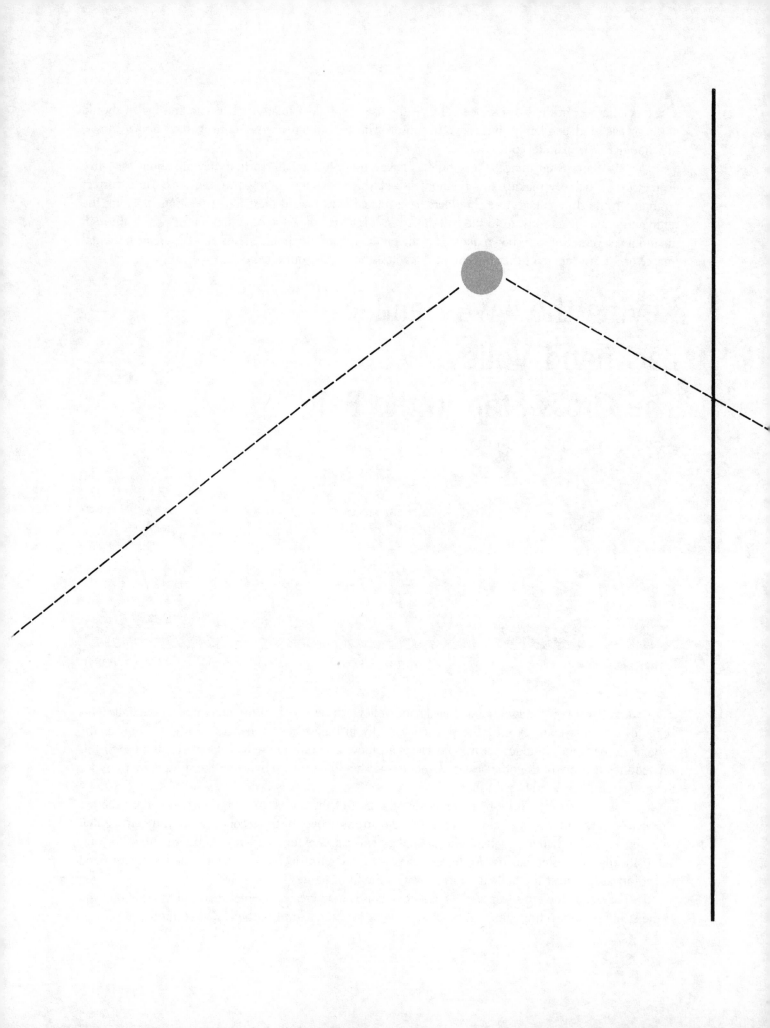

THE SERVE

*T*here is a saying in tennis: you are only as good as your serve. In match play, if you hold your serve, the worst that can happen is that every set will go to a tiebreaker. And, if you hold your serve, with just one service break, you would win every set. All great players have the capacity to win most of their service games as a matter of routine. The ability to hold serve at higher and higher levels of competition is usually what determines how far a player can progress competitively in the game.

Unfortunately, at the recreational level, the opposite is often true: many players are only as bad as their serves. They are unable to hold serve on a consistent basis, and are under continuous pressure to break serve just to stay even in the match. Often they hit the first serve as hard and as flat as possible. But since it rarely goes in, they are reduced to a tentative, pushed second serve. This destroys the advantage of serving. It allows the opponent to take the offensive from the first ball. It turns what should be the most positive aspect of the game into an immediate liability.

There is a certain confidence and sense of rhythm that comes from playing consistent service games. Knowing that he can serve effectively, the player's focus shifts to putting together the necessary shot combinations to break his opponent. Once this is achieved, the remainder of the match can be played almost on automatic pilot.

Most recreational players, and many competitive players as well, never approach this frame of mind. There are many reasons why this is true, but as in the case of the other basic shots in the game, good serving can be boiled down to one factor—consistent technical execution. And of all the strokes in the game, the serve is probably the one which most players execute the most poorly.

In one fundamental way, the serve differs from every other shot in tennis. When you serve, you are not hitting an oncoming ball. Rather than reacting to a speeding ball directed at you by an opponent, you are, instead, hitting a ball that has no oncoming velocity—it is virtually hanging in the air in front of you. Since the server starts the point with the ball in his hand, nothing happens until he makes it happen himself.

Most players, however, fail to realize what this absence of oncoming ball velocity means in terms of the bio-mechanics of the motion. In the case of a groundstroke or a volley, the oncoming velocity of the ball means that at contact, there is a significant impact. Even though there should be a feeling of smoothness and relaxation to these strokes, there is a certain level of muscle tension required to withstand the impact. But there is no similar collision between the racket and the ball on the serve. In the other strokes, a large part of the speed of the shot comes from the force already present in the oncoming ball. With the serve, there is no oncoming velocity. The goal, instead, is to generate this initial velocity through the service motion. To do this requires greater racket head acceleration than on the groundstrokes or volleys. And the key to maximizing the racket head acceleration on the serve is a relaxed, full motion.

Unfortunately, few recreational players approach the service motion with these facts in mind. They are used to the level of muscle tension required for groundstrokes, and simply carry this feeling over into the service motion. Or worse, in an attempt to increase the speed of the serve, they tense up and muscle the ball even *more*. The result is a stiff, constricted motion, and an actual reduction in the pace generated.

If you look at the path of the racket on the serve, you will see that it is more than twice as long as the swing on the groundstrokes, and takes at least twice as long to execute. This long, full motion produces maximum racket head acceleration at the contact point, and is the primary power source on the serve. In addition to the swing path, there are two sources of additional power:

the rotation of the shoulders and the body into the shot, and the uncoiling action of the legs.

The second power source, body rotation, will happen automatically, provided that the player begins the motion with the shoulders positioned correctly. As the photo sequences will demonstrate, the motion should begin with the shoulders perpendicular to the net. This is analogous to the correct position of the shoulders at the completion of the Turn on the groundstrokes. As with the groundstrokes, the correct shoulder rotation will then occur naturally as a consequence of the swing pattern. Most recreational players, however, unknowingly eliminate this automatic power source from the game by standing incorrectly in the Ready Position.

The full value of shoulder rotation as a power source in the service motion can be seen by examining the delivery of John McEnroe. Though many observers have labeled his serve unorthodox, or at least, idiosyncratic, the truth is it represents a significant advance in the bio-mechanics of the motion. What sets McEnroe's serve apart is his distinctive sideways stance. This stance confuses critics, and is what has led to this misunderstanding of what actually happens during his motion. In fact, if McEnroe were to start his motion from the traditional position, it would appear flawlessly classical. But, by standing with both feet parallel along the edge of the baseline, McEnroe adds a new dimension to the concept of body leverage in the serve. The fact is, with the sideways stance, McEnroe actually doubles the role of the shoulders in the execution of the motion. When McEnroe starts his forward motion to the ball, his back is literally turned to the net. Unlike the standard motion in which the shoulders rotate a maximum of 90 degrees, McEnroe achieves almost twice that, or nearly 180 degrees of shoulder rotation throughout the course of the motion. The result is tremendous additional power, and ball rotation.

Advanced students of the game may want to experiment with the sideways stance after they have developed full control of the other aspects of the service motion. The vast majority of players, however, can learn something from McEnroe simply by developing full shoulder rotation within the context of the classical motion. This means standing with the front foot parallel to the baseline, and the shoulders perpendicular to the net. If you watch pro tennis on television, you will notice how many of the top players known for their serves start in this position.

After the shoulders, the third and final power source in the service motion is the legs. The topic of the correct leg work on the serve is also a debated one, with opinion divided into two primary viewpoints. The older view, a standard in the library of tennis tips, is that, to maximize power on the serve, you should step through the shot with the back, right leg. This was the pattern followed by many of the great Australian champions in the 1960s and early 1970s, and also by a small number of the current top players.

In my opinion, this is the single worst mistake made by recreational players on the serve, because stepping through the ball with the back right foot on the serve destroys the timing of the body rotation. It gets the hips and the shoulders out of sync with the racket. They rotate too soon, so that by the time the racket gets to the ball, a significant amount of the potential body leverage is wasted. In addition, the step and the premature rotation make it impossible to coil the knees fully, the real source of additional power on the serve. Stepping through the shot on the serve would be the equivalent of stepping through the groundstrokes with the back foot. Imagine the loss of timing and body leverage if you stepped to the ball with the back *right* foot on the forehand!

The whole idea behind the step theory is to get the body into the shot. In reality, this can be accomplished only by relying on the legs and knees. The principle is the same as for the groundstrokes: coil the quadriceps by maximizing the knee bend. This allows them to release into the ball as a natural consequence of the swing. A player who uses his knees in this fashion will automatically spring upward into the ball. When the knees are properly coiled, rather than cross stepping with the back foot, the player will land on the front foot, and the back leg will kick away from the body for balance. This footwork pattern is sometimes called the thrust, or the hop. It is easily the dominant technique on the pro tour. Examples of players who use it include most of the great servers in the game: John McEnroe, Ivan Lendl, Stefan Edberg, Martina Navratilova, and Steffi Graf, among others.

Another debated issue in serving theory is ball toss. This subject has also been widely misunderstood, to the great detriment of vast numbers of recreational players. According to the predominant tennis tip theory, the correct toss should be low, so that the player strikes the ball at the top of the toss, or even on the way up. The player usually cited as a model for the perfect toss by this school is Roscoe Tanner, a top American player in the 1970s and early 1980s. Although he never won a Grand Slam title, Tanner was widely known for the tremendous velocity of his serve, clocked on radar at over 140 miles per hour. This velocity was indeed due in part to his extremely low service toss. Because the toss was low, Tanner was forced to execute the service motion very rapidly, and this in turn led to increased racket head speed and his famous ball velocity.

There are, however, many problems with this theory. First, to execute the motion so quickly, it is crucial that the player stay extremely loose and relaxed. As noted above, this is already a major difficulty for any player on the serve. The low toss tends to compound the problem. The average player, in his anxiety to get the racket around, tends to tense up even more, preventing the very effect he is hoping to accomplish. A related problem with the low toss is the need for superior timing, to get the racket head positioned correctly at contact in so brief an interval. Even a slight error in the angle of the racket head at contact can produce an inaccurate delivery, and thus become a fundamental cause of inconsistency. These factors of relaxation and timing plagued Tanner under the pressure of big matches (for example, his Wimbledon final loss to Bjorn Borg in 1979) when his percentage of first serves dropped dramatically.

According to the low toss argument, a higher ball toss is much more difficult to time. This is true, allegedly, because as the ball starts to drop down, it begins to accelerate, and this change in speed makes timing the contact difficult. But this is a ridiculous claim. The speed of the ball during the toss is a fraction of the velocity of an oncoming groundstroke. A player who is struggling with his timing on his serve because of a low toss often has no trouble timing oncoming shots that are traveling with great velocity. On the toss the ball is moving at a fraction of this speed. Any player capable of rallying the ball at even a very low pace has more than enough hand-eye coordination to time the speed of the ball on the service toss.

In reality a high service toss is actually much easier to time. The real problem is having enough time to execute the motion smoothly and with technical precision. Again, the swing path on the serve is more than twice the length of the groundstrokes. To complete the motion correctly takes time, and it is the height of the toss that gives the player the chance to do this. Therefore, a high toss is a primary key to developing an effective serve. If you doubt this, take a quick look at the ball tosses on the tour. The overwhelming majority of professional players have high tosses, and hit the ball somewhere on the way down. There is not a single player on the tour today with a toss as low as Roscoe Tanner's. McEnroe has one of the lower tosses among the top players, but his ball typically drops six inches to a foot before contact. Other players, such as Lendl, Edberg, and Becker, toss the ball much higher than McEnroe, with Lendl about two feet higher than the contact point. If these players need a high toss in order to execute their service motions, how much more so the majority of tournament and recreational players.

A high toss is crucial for a successful serve. The only real issue is *how high* the toss should be. The key to answering this question is the personal rhythm of the individual server. Every player has a slightly different rhythm to his delivery. The trick is to find the toss that suits it best. Some players can move through the motion relatively quickly, stay relaxed, and keep the delivery smooth. Others need more time, and move through the backswing at a significantly slower pace. The slower your natural windup, the higher your toss should be. The correct pace for your serve can be determined only by experimentation and feel. As a rule of thumb, you should start by tossing about a foot above the contact point and evaluate the results. If you feel rushed and tense, give yourself additional time by tossing higher. If you feel you are waiting for the ball, and your racket is lagging, then lower the toss a little until you find the right tempo.

Finally, there is the question of service grip. Although there are occasional exceptions, most players should learn the basic motion for the serve with their forehand grip. This will produce a flat shot, but the player will develop a basic feeling for the motion, for striking the ball solidly, and for controlling the direction of the shot. Initially, the focus should be on establishing the correct technical swing path.

Once the basic swing is consistent, the player can change to a true serving grip and can begin to develop spin. Unfortunately, a great many recreational players never make this step, although hitting with spin is absolutely essential in developing an effective serve. They wind up with a hard, flat first serve that rarely goes in, and a weak second serve that opponents routinely attack. As with the groundstrokes, spin on the serve causes the ball to arc rather than travel in a straight line. This means more net clearance, and a ball that will drop more sharply down into the service box. By hitting with spin, the player is able to hit the ball harder and still have confidence that the serve will be in. On the second serve, this confidence is vital. By increasing the amount of rotation on the ball, the player ensures that he will hit this critical shot with unfailing consistency.

There are two keys to developing spin. The first, as I have noted, is the grip. There are two variations of the serve grip that are widely used. One is the full backhand grip. The second, which is more comfortable and effective for most players, is the continental. These are demonstrated in the grip chapter. By simply changing to a service grip and executing the same basic motion, the player will automatically generate spin. This is because the grip change will alter the angle at which the racket face strikes the ball, causing the strings to brush across the back of the ball.

The second factor in the creation of spin is the angle of the racket head movement when it strikes the ball. Typically, the types of spin on the serve are described as either "slice" or "topspin." In reality, the type of spin is really a matter of degree. If the racket head is traveling across in more of a horizontal line, the serve will have more sidespin, the ball will move from right to left, and will have a little less kick, and will bounce lower, after it hits the court. Typically, this rotation is described as a slice serve. McEnroe's serve is a good example of this variation. If, on the other hand, the angle of the diagonal is more vertical, so that the racket head is moving more sharply upward at contact, then the ball will travel in a straighter path, but will dip more sharply, and will tend to kick or bounce higher upon contact with the court. This is the topspin serve.

For most players, the topspin variation will probably be the easiest to master, and the most effective. The increased arc makes it a higher percentage stroke. The spin produces more net clearance and the dipping action brings the ball down into the service box. Furthermore, the higher bounce creates problems for opponents on the return. With this spin, the ball can be kicked up to shoulder level or even higher, forcing the returning player to hit a high, weak return. His only effective counterplay is to take the ball on the rise, before it can get up and on top of him. Since this is a difficult return to time consistently, and is also a likely source of errors, it generates free points for the server.

With the basic motion and use of spin described in this chapter, the difference between the first serve and the second serve is primarily a matter of degree. The first ball can be hit slightly flatter, and thus with a little more pace. The second ball should have more rotation—giving the player complete confidence in his ability to place the ball in the box, even under the pressure of big points. As described above, however, most players have a consistent tendency to overhit the first serve. It may be going 100 miles an hour, but that is of little benefit if it never goes into the court. Players who cannot achieve a first serve percentage of 65 to 75 percent should increase the rotation on their first ball to achieve this consistency. They may discover that this delivery leads to winning more service games more easily.

According to one school of thought, every player should develop the ability to hit both a topspin and a slice serve. This school also advocates changing the toss for the different spins. Thus, a slice toss should be more to the right of the server, and possibly lower, making it easier to hit around the side of the ball. The toss for the topspin serve should be further back to the left, slightly over the server's head, so that the player can hit up on the ball more radically for topspin. Again, if we look at the top players, we can see that none of them hit two distinct types of spin, much less have two different ball tosses. In the first place, making such a basic change in the motion from ball to ball is prohibitively difficult. The serve requires the rhythmic coordination of the toss and the motion of the body. It is difficult enough to develop one consistent service delivery, let alone two. In the second place, an experienced player will quickly learn to read changes in the placement of the toss, and will then know what serve you are planning to hit almost as soon as you do yourself. This will drastically reduce, if not completely eliminate, any advantage in alternating between two spins.

Instead of having two different service motions, top players develop variations in the *degree of spin*. These can be hit off the same toss, with the exact same motion. The variation in the amount of spin comes from altering the spot on which the racket makes contact with the ball, and the angle of the diagonal along which the racket head is moving, not by making a fundamental change in the service motion itself. By using the same toss for every serve, the player makes it difficult for an opponent to read his delivery. By following this approach, a player will actually develop *three* service variations, not two. He will be able to hit the first serve fairly flat, and also, with moderate spin. In addition, he will be able to hit the second ball with heavier rotation. This heavier spin can also be mixed with the other two varieties on the first serve, to keep the opponent guessing and off balance, or if the server finds that his opponent has trouble with the higher bounce. This will be the case more often than most players realize. Some players will hit much better returns off flat, hard serves. Unless a server can generate enough velocity to overpower his opponents, hitting flat deliveries may actually be counterproductive. This is particularly true when playing serve and volley tennis, when hard servers frequently find themselves scraping bullet returns off their shoe laces on the first volley. The ball with heavier spin, on the other hand, travels slightly slower, so it allows the net rusher to close to the net faster, as well as forcing higher, floating returns that are much easier to volley.

In this chapter, the process of learning to serve with the proper mix of power, control, and spin is divided into stages. The first is the mastery of the swing pattern. This is presented in the basic serve sequence photos and teaching progressions. The second step is developing the ability to hit moderate spin, staying within the framework of the basic motion. This is presented as a variation on the basic serve sequence. The third step is learning to hit with heavier ball rotation. Finally, the fourth step is adding advanced footwork, the leg thrust described above, and the source of the superior power of the great servers in modern game. This is demonstrated in a second still photo sequence. Following the progressions, it is possible for any player to bring his serve up to the level of the other parts of his game, and learn to win serve on a regular basis in both recreational and tournament play.

CREATING THE SWING PATTERN FOR THE BASIC SERVE

In this chapter, you will use the principles of visualization to learn the swing pattern for the basic serve. As with all the other strokes, you will learn a physical and visual model of the motion, using a combination of sequence photos and text. The model, in turn, will become your personal blueprint for developing a solid and effective serve.

First, the motion is shown from the front view, broken down into its component frames, and its general technical characteristics are outlined. Then the stroke is presented from the front and side views simultaneously, and the key still frames are identified. Because of the longer, more complex swing pattern required, there are six key still frames on the serve, versus four still frames for groundstrokes and volleys. These still frames are:

1. **The Ready Position**
2. **The Toss**
3. **The Backswing**
4. **The Racket Drop**
5. **The Contact Point**
6. **The Finish Position**

The still frames are the basis for mastering the physical and visual models. Note that, as with the groundstrokes and the volleys, if the player passes through each of the still frames correctly, this will guarantee that the entire swing pattern is correct as well.

The next section shows you how to learn each of the six still frames for the serve, by teaching you the checkpoints. The following section shows you how to do muscle memory corrections for the serve. The key section teaches you how to develop your own system of stroke keys for producing the serve consistently in rallies and match play. Finally, the advanced serve, which maximizes the use of the legs for additional power and spin, is presented as a variation, along with the necessary additional keys.

1	2	3	4	5
READY POSITION	ARM DROP	TOSS POSITION	BACKSWING	START OF RACKET DROP

Characteristics of the Basic Serve
FRONT VIEW

○ ○

Grip: To learn the basic motion, start with your forehand grip, unless it is a severe modified eastern grip, in which case it is probably easier to start with a grip closer to the pure eastern. As soon as the player has mastered the basic swing and developed a feel for solid contact with the forehand grip, he should progress to the continental grip to develop spin, as explained later in this chapter. The continental grip is demonstrated in the grip chapter.

Full Motion: Compared with the groundstrokes, the basic swing pattern on the serve is twice as long. It starts with the racket pointing straight at the net (Frame 1). The arms drop down together (Frame 2), and then go up together until the hitting arm is completely straight and pointing directly at the back fence (Frame 3). The racket movement continues upward until it points directly up (Frame 4), and then drops all the way down the back (Frame 6). From there the hitting arm snaps the racket up to the Contact Point at full extension (Frame 8). The followthrough is all the way across the body, ending

6	7	8	9	10	11
RACKET DROP	**START OF HIT**	**CONTACT POINT**	**FOLLOWTHROUGH**		**FINISH POSITION**

when the racket hand touches down on the front of the left leg (Frame 11). This full swing path is the primary power source in the motion.

High Toss: A key aspect to the successful execution of the motion is a high toss. The toss allows the player time to reach full extension at the Contact Point, extending as fully as possible from the tip of the toes to the tip of the racket (Frame 8). It also allows him to develop a smooth, relaxed rhythm, and maximize the acceleration of the racket head. The height should be a minimum of six inches to a foot higher than the actual contact, so that the player hits the ball slightly on the way down. The toss should also be to the right and in front of the body, so that the Contact Point is directly above the right shoulder, and in front of the left front foot. The key to a consistent toss is keeping the tossing arm straight. It is straight in the Ready Position (Frame 1), as it drops down to the leg (Frame 2), and at the ball release (Frame 3). At the completion of the Backswing (Frame 4), it is still straight and fully extended.

Additional Power Sources: After a complete swing path, the second power source is shoulder rotation. If the serve starts with the shoulders in the correct position perpendicular to the net (Frame 1), the rotation is produced automatically in the course of the swing. At the start of the upward hitting motion (Frame 7), the shoulders have already begun to rotate into the shot. This continues through the course of the motion, so that the shoulders are parallel to the net at the finish, and have rotated a full ninety degrees. The final power source is the legs. Note that at the completion of the Backswing (Frame 4), the weight is fully shifted forward to the left, front foot, and the knees are coiled. From this position the legs release into the shot as a natural consequence of hitting motion (Frames 5–7).

Basic Serve:
Six Key Still Frames · SIDE VIEW

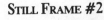

STILL FRAME #1   ### STILL FRAME #2   ### STILL FRAME #3

READY POSITION ARM DROP   TOSS POSITION   BACKSWING   START OF
                                                                       RACKET DROP

Basic Serve:
Six Key Still Frames · FRONT VIEW

STILL FRAME #1   ### STILL FRAME #2   ### STILL FRAME #3

READY POSITION   ARM DROP   TOSS POSITION   BACKSWING   START OF
                                                                        RACKET DROP

184

STILL FRAME #4   STILL FRAME #5   STILL FRAME #6

RACKET DROP   START OF HIT   CONTACT POINT   FOLLOWTHROUGH   FINISH POSITION

STILL FRAME #5

STILL FRAME #4   STILL FRAME #6

RACKET DROP   START OF HIT   CONTACT POINT   FOLLOWTHROUGH   FINISH POSITION

Still Frame 1
The Ready Position

○ ○ ○ ○ ○ ○ ○ ○ ○ ○ ○ ○ ○ ○ ○ ○ ○ ○ ○

Checkpoints:

1. *The Shoulders:* The shoulders start perpendicular to the net in the Ready Position. The player stands straight up and down from the waist. The knees are slightly flexed.

2. *The Hitting Arm:* The hitting arm is straight, and hangs down from the shoulder so that it is in line with the front leg. The basic serve can be executed with either the forehand or the continental grip.

3. *The Racket:* The tip of the racket points straight at net. The shaft of the racket is parallel with the court, and the face is perpendicular. The left, tossing arm is straight, and the ball is on the face of the racket.

4. *The Legs:* The feet are sideways, parallel to the baseline, with the heels in line. The weight is equally distributed on both feet, and knees are slightly flexed.

Establish the position physically using the checkpoints, then create the mental image.

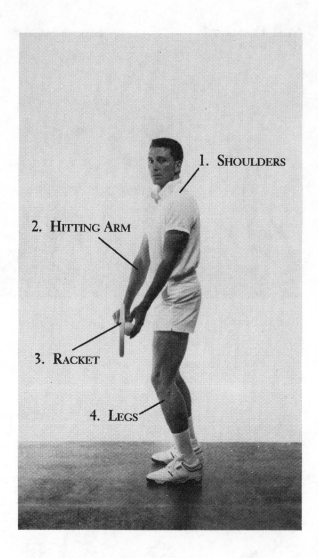

1. SHOULDERS

2. HITTING ARM

3. RACKET

4. LEGS

Still Frame 2
The Toss

○ ○ ○ ○ ○ ○ ○ ○ ○ ○

Checkpoints:

1. The Shoulders: The shoulders have remained perpendicular to the net. The left tossing arm is straight and has dropped straight down to the front of the left leg on the hinge of the shoulder. From there, the tossing arm moves straight upward releasing the ball at about shoulder height.

2. The Hitting Arm: The hitting arm has traced a perfect half circle from the Ready Position until it points directly back at the back fence. The arm has not gone back behind the plane of the body, but is still on the right side of the shoulders.

3. The Racket: The racket now points straight back at the back fence as well. It has traced the circumference of a half circle. The face of the racket has turned over at the bottom of the arm.

4. The Legs: The weight has started to shift forward to the left front foot. The knee bend has increased, particularly in the front left leg as the weight is transferred.

Start in the Ready Position and move to the Toss. Establish the position physically by using the checkpoints, then create the mental image.

Still Frame 3
The Backswing

○ ○ ○ ○ ○ ○ ○ ○ ○ ○ ○

Checkpoints:

1. The Shoulders: The shoulders have remained in their original perpendicular position. The body is straight up and down from the waist. The left tossing arm is still straight and fully extended.

2. The Hitting Arm: The upper arm is still pointing back at the back fence, but the elbow has started to bend, so that the forearm points directly up at the sky.

3. The Racket: The shaft of the racket is also pointing directly up, and the face of the racket is still vertical to the court. In effect, the tip of the racket has traced a path that is three fourths of the circumference of a circle.

4. The Legs: The weight has now fully shifted to the left front leg, and the knee bend is maximized. The player has started to come up on his back toes. Note that there has been no stepping motion with the back foot.

Start in the Ready Position. Move through the Toss to the Backswing. Establish the position physically using the checkpoints, then create the mental image.

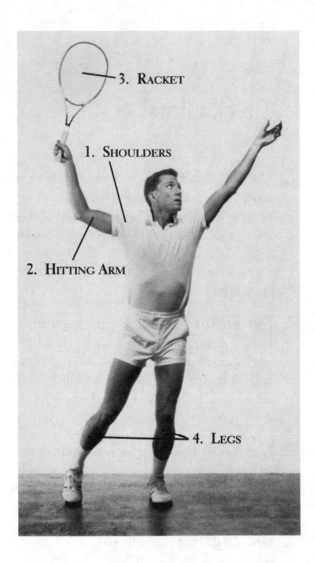

Still Frame 4
The Racket Drop

○ ○ ○ ○ ○ ○ ○ ○ ○ ○ ○ ○ ○

Checkpoints:

1. *The Shoulders:* At the Racket Drop, the shoulders remain sideways or perpendicular, and the player is still straight up and down from the waist.

2. *The Hitting Arm:* The hitting arm has relaxed and bent at the elbow, so that the racket can fully drop. The elbow position is high, about thirty degrees above the perpendicular position at the completion of the Backswing.

3. *The Racket:* The racket has dropped all the way down the back. The edge of the racket is in position to scratch the center of the spine. The tip of the racket is pointing directly down at the court.

4. *The Legs:* The weight is still forward on the left front foot. The knees have started to release naturally as a consequence of the motion.

Move from the Ready Position through the still frames to the Racket Drop. Establish the position physically using the checkpoints, then create the mental image.

Still Frame 5
The Contact Point

○ ○ ○ ○ ○ ○ ○ ○ ○ ○ ○ ○ ○ ○ ○

Checkpoints:

1. *The Shoulders:* The shoulders have started to rotate with the start of the hitting motion, and are at about forty-five degrees to the net. The power from the rotation is transferred naturally into the ball, as an automatic consequence of the proper stance and swing. The upper body is straight up and down from the waist.

2. *The Hitting Arm:* The forearm has snapped the racket up to the Contact Point from the elbow. The arm is straight, and fully extended upward from the shoulder.

3. *The Racket:* The racket head is directly above the right shoulder and slightly in front of the front foot, so that the contact is over the court and in front of the body. The shaft of the racket is perpendicular to the court.

4. *The Legs:* The knees have released from their coiled position upward into the ball, but are still slightly flexed. The weight is on the front foot, and the player is starting to come up on the back toes. The player has not stepped through the shot, and remains on balance.

Start in the Ready Position, and move through the still frames to the Contact Point. Establish the position physically using the checkpoints, then create the mental image.

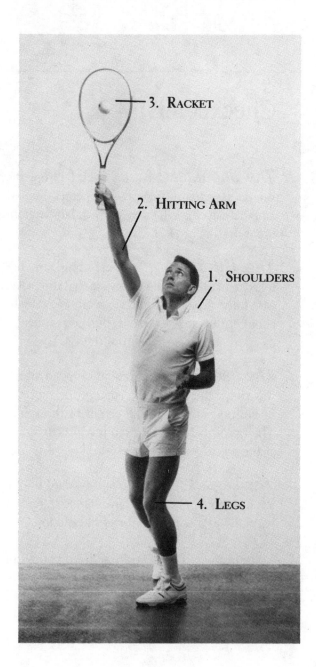

3. RACKET

2. HITTING ARM

1. SHOULDERS

4. LEGS

Still Frame 6
The Finish Position

○○○○○○○○○○○○○○

Checkpoints:

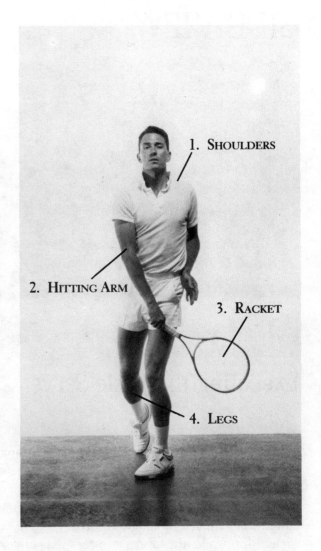

1. **The Shoulders:** The shoulders have rotated a full ninety degrees from the Ready Position until they are parallel with the net. The upper body has remained straight up and down from the waist.

2. **The Hitting Arm:** The hitting arm has remained relaxed, carrying the racket all the way through to the finish in a smooth motion. The right racket hand should touch down in the middle of the left front leg.

3. **The Racket:** The racket has accelerated all the way through the hit. The racket head moves out along the line of the shot, and then down and across the body. At the finish the racket is on the left side of the left front leg.

4. **The Legs:** The weight is now fully forward on the left front foot, and the player has come up on his right toes for balance. The knees have uncoiled into the ball, but remain slightly flexed.

Start in the Ready Position, and move all the way through the still frames to the Finish Position. Establish the position physically using the checkpoints, then create the mental image.

Putting the Still Frames Together
SIDE VIEW

○ ○ ○ ○ ○ ○ ○ ○ ○ ○ ○ ○ ○ ○ ○ ○ ○ ○ ○ ○

READY   TOSS   BACKSWING   RACKET   CONTACT   FINISH
POSITION   POSITION   DROP   POINT   POSITION

Executing the Basic Serve

After you are comfortable with the six still frames and the checkpoints for the basic serve, the next step is to put them together into a full swing pattern as shown.

Start in the Ready Position. Drop your arms and shift the weight forward to the left, front foot. As the motion starts, the hitting arm drops down and points down at the court, then turns over and moves backward and upward to the Toss Position, along the edge of the circumference of an imaginary circle. Meanwhile, the tossing arm goes straight down to the front of the leg, and then straight up. The ball release is at about shoulder level. Next, move the racket upward to the Backswing position. The tip of the racket points up toward the sky, and the upper arm is still horizontal to the court. The tossing arm is now fully extended. Relax the arm and let it drop all the way down the back. From here the forearm snaps the racket up to full extension. The Contact Point is high, above the shoulder and slightly to the right, and also, slightly in front of the plane of the body. Finally, the motion finishes with the hitting arm and racket following through all the way across the body. The whole motion should be relaxed and executed much more slowly and with less muscle tension than the groundstrokes or volleys.

Start the development of your muscle memory with practice swings—executing the motion without actually hitting balls. As you pass through the individual still frames, make sure that each checkpoint is correct. If you are unsure, stop and verify the checkpoints for the particular still frame. As with the other strokes, if each still frame is correct, this virtually guarantees that the entire motion will be correct as well. Build up to ten swings. If possible, do this work in front of a mirror.

Next, progress to controlled drill. For the serve, this means using as many practice balls as possible. A minimum is about 20, although about 100 balls is ideal. Some clubs and tennis centers will let you use their teaching balls for this purpose. Start serving in the add court. This makes it easier to align the shoulders in the correct perpendicular position in the Ready Position. Initially, it is not important that the ball goes in the court on every serve, rather your goal is to develop a feeling for the correct technical motion. As you become comfortable with the swing, the ball will start to find the service box automatically, and with increasing frequency.

Many beginning players find that executing the complete motion poses problems, at least initially. If this is true for you, you should wind up *before* the ball Toss. Progress through the still frames and stop in the Racket Drop Position. Now toss the ball, and execute the rest of the motion. If you are a more advanced player who has problems making a full Racket Drop, you should follow this procedure as well, and wind up before the Toss. Once your execution is correct using the two-part motion, you can begin to put the serve together into one continuous movement.

Once you can execute the motion consistently in controlled drill, you can serve practice points. The best way to do achieve confidence doing this is to play what are called "no double fault" points with a practice partner. This means that you serve however many balls are required—one, two, twenty, or whatever—to get the ball in the box, with correct technical form. This removes the fear of double faulting, and the tendency to abandon the correct technical motion and push the second serve in the box. Once the server gets a good serve in, the partner returns the ball, and the point is played out. Now the server goes to the other court and the process is repeated. Most players who play these no double fault points quickly find that they regularly get at least one of two serves in the box anyway. This process should give you the confidence to execute the correct motion under the pressure of the double fault. Once the serve is consistent playing practice points, you should progress to match play.

As with the other strokes, the final aspect of developing deep muscle memory on the serve is to practice visualizing the motion away from the court. You can do this by setting aside visual practice time, or simply utilizing spare moments in the course of the day. Visualize the entire stroke pattern, and as you develop your stroke key system as outlined below, practice visualizing the keys that are active for you. Have yourself videotaped executing the serve correctly in controlled drill, and watch this as well as instructional footage of correct serving technique.

As explained in the introduction, most players master the basic elements of the motion more easily by beginning with some version of a forehand grip. As soon as the motion is solid, however, they should add spin to their delivery. The process for doing this is presented in the key section. If the biomechanics are established, this is relatively simple to achieve, requiring only a grip change, and a slight alteration in the racket swing path prior to contact.

The final step in maximizing the potential of the serve is to develop advanced footwork. This allows the player to make use of the legs, adding tremendous additional power and spin. The advanced serve is presented as a variation in the last section of the chapter.

Muscle Memory Corrections

○ ○

As with the volleys, the role of muscle memory correction is less central in developing the serve than the groundstrokes. This is because of the crucial role of the Racket Drop, and of the Contact Point. However, there are several common errors that can be quickly eliminated by the use of muscle memory correction. They are demonstrated below.

The process for doing this is the same as with the other strokes. At the conclusion of the stroke, the player simply freezes in the statueman position. Instead of recovering, he stops and compares his actual position to the checkpoints for the correct finish. Next, he moves directly from wherever he actually is to where he should have been if he had followed the pattern correctly. This process teaches the muscles the difference between an error and the right technical motion, and increases the probability the next serve will follow the pattern more accurately. Over time, the correction process will bring the stroke and the model closely in line. As with the groundstrokes and the volleys, you should make regular use of video. By watching video of your actual stroke production, you will not only see how you are deviating from your model, you will develop the clearest possible image of the model stroke.

The three most common errors at the finish on the basic serve are finishing with a short followthrough, stepping through the ball with the back foot, and bending over at the waist in the course of the motion. All three errors typically result from trying to generate additional pace at the expense of proper technique. They are demonstrated below, along with the corrections to eliminate them from your game. Do these corrections while you are working on your serve in controlled drill. Stop every five balls, evaluate your position, and adjust to the right finish using the checkpoints. Over time the corrections will become smaller and smaller, and your motion will follow the model more precisely and consistently.

Muscle Memory Correction: Followthrough

A common tendency on the serve is to overhit the ball by tightening the arm muscles and stopping short on the followthrough in a misguided effort to generate additional power. In reality, the short followthrough creates a power loss. Real power is generated by racket head speed, and racket head speed is maximized by a full, fluid motion. Also, without a full followthrough, there is a corresponding reduction in spin, which is also dependent on the speed of the racket head as it brushes the ball.

To check the followthrough and correct any errors, freeze in the statueman position at the end of the stroke. Using the checkpoints, reposition your arm and racket as shown. The racket hand should finish fully across the body, touching down on the left, front leg.

STATUEMAN
Short Followthrough
and Correction

ERROR: SHORT FOLLOWTHROUGH   CORRECTED FINISH POSITION

Muscle Memory Correction:
Leg Position

One of the most common errors in club tennis is the tendency to "step through" the serve in the hope that this will get the body into the shot, or start the serve and volley player on his way to the net more quickly. In fact, stepping with the back foot causes the hips and shoulders to rotate through the motion too soon, throwing off the natural release of body leverage. In the extreme case, it can cause the player to get himself ahead of the toss, so that the contact is behind the plane of the body. The correct method for maximizing body leverage is not by stepping through the shot, but by coiling and releasing the knees, as shown in the section on advanced serve. Hitting off a solid base on the basic serve lays the foundation for developing this more advanced footwork.

To correct this error, freeze in the statueman position, and check the position of your legs. If you have stepped through, reposition your feet as shown, using the checkpoints for the Finish Position.

ERROR: STEPPING THROUGH WITH THE BACK FOOT   CORRECTED FINISH POSITION

Muscle Memory Correction:
Body Position

Another common error on the basic motion is the tendency to bend at the waist. Again, this a result of trying to overhit the ball by throwing the shoulders forward in the course of the hitting motion. Instead of additional power, the bend results in a lower Contact Point and less net clearance. The player cuts his body leverage in half, eliminating to a great extent the role of the hips and legs in transferring power into the shot.

To correct this error, freeze in the statueman position, and adjust your body until you are standing straight up and down from the waist. This will allow you to reach full extension at contact, and allow the automatic generation of body leverage.

STATUEMAN
Bending at the Waist
and Correction

ERROR: BEND FROM THE WAIST   CORRECTED FINISH POSITION

KEYING
THE BASIC SERVE

As with each of the basic strokes, the final step in mastering the basic serve is to create your own system of stroke keys. By visualizing a key while on the court, the player activates the entire stroke pattern. The keys presented here will provide you with a reliable method for serving well in match play. They also provide the antidote for difficult technical problems that many players have been unable to remedy through traditional lessons.

In this section, six different keys are presented. The first key is for the timing of the motion. Assuming the swing pattern is correct, the biggest problem most players face is developing and maintaining the slower rhythm of the stroke, particularly in the excitement of matches. This key shows you how to key the timing of the motion to a three count that will keep the rhythm smooth. The next three keys are images of the still frames, all shown from the player's perspective: the Racket Drop, the Contact Point, and the Finish Position. These keys are not only effective in producing consistent execution, but can also be used to correct certain technical problems with the swing itself, as explained below.

The fifth key is for the tossing motion. Without a good toss, it is simply impossible to hit the serve correctly, and for many players, the toss is the single most difficult obstacle. Finally, the last key shows you how to generate spin on the basic serve once the fundamental motion is solid. This is the key to serving aggressively in tennis. Spin gives a player the confidence that he can get both his first and second serve in the court, even under pressure, without having to hold back the motion. It allows the player to have confidence that he can hit out on the serve and actually increase his serving percentages and accuracy. The learning procedure for creating your stroke keys is identical to that for mastering the still frames. First, establish the key physically, referring to the checkpoints that accompany the image. Next, close your eyes and create an image of the key in your mind's eye, giving it as much detail as possible. Notice how it feels physically, and make the image and the feeling correspond in your mind. Then test the key in controlled drill. As you start your service motion, hold the image of the key in your mind, and make the motion overlap the image.

If you visualize the key clearly, it should result in the correct execution of the entire service motion. Hit ten or twenty balls in controlled drill. If the key produces consistent serves, then it is an active key. Progress to practice points and match play and test the key there. You may also find that slight variations of the key are more effective. For example, rather than using the entire still frame, you may want to visualize just one aspect of the image.

The keys presented here should be used as a guide in developing your own personal system of serve keys. Your goal is to determine which keys are active, and which counteract your own particular tendencies. Correlate your errors with the counteracting keys. Test the keys, and others that you may discover, in controlled drill, rallies, and in match play. Compile your stroke key chart from the results of this work, and update it as required.

Keying the Basic Serve: The Three Count

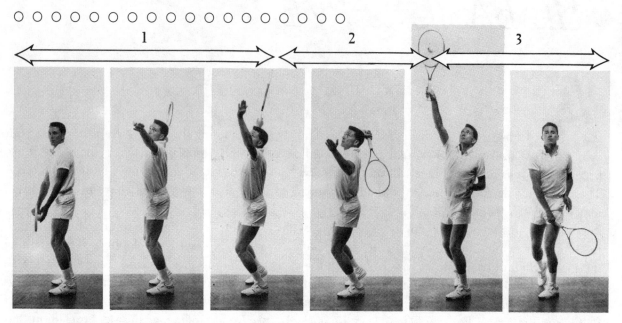

THE COORDINATION OF THE PARTS OF THE SERVICE MOTION WITH THE RHYTHM OF THE THREE COUNT.

The best key for keeping the rhythm of the motion even, and thus keeping the arm relaxed, is the use of the three count. Start in the Ready Position. Now, as you start the motion, count to yourself "one, two, three." The count should be slow and even. "One" should correspond, roughly, with the Arm Drop, and the start of the Backswing. Count "two" as the Backswing continues and the racket drops behind the back. "Three" corresponds with the start of motion upward to the ball, the contact, and the followthrough.

The problem most players face is that, somewhere between two and three, they tense up the arm and try to speed up the motion artificially, rather than allowing it to accelerate naturally. This constricts the flow of the movement and reduces racket head speed. By keeping the rhythm of the count even, you will keep the rhythm of the serve even as well. This will maximize the speed of your swing.

There is an interrelationship between the height of the toss and the rhythm of the service motion. Some players will find that they can move through the motion fairly quickly, stay relaxed, and keep the rhythm even. Other players find that if they move too quickly, they inevitably tense up too much, and rush the motion, particularly between "two" and "three." The slower your own individual rhythm, the higher you need to toss the ball. The exact height and the exact correspondence between the three count and the parts of the motion are something you must determine through experimentation. A rule of thumb is to start by tossing six inches to a foot above your Contact Point, and then to evaluate your rhythm. If you feel rushed, increase the height of the toss. If you feel that you are waiting to hit the ball, then lower the toss slightly. To create this key, start in the Ready Position. Now close your eyes and count to yourself. As you count, visualize yourself executing the serve motion, in synchronization with the count. Now test the key in controlled drill.

Keying the Basic Serve: The Racket Drop

○ ○ ○ ○ ○ ○ ○ ○ ○ ○ ○ ○ ○ ○ ○ ○ ○ ○ ○ ○

The primary power source on the service motion is the snap of the racket up to the contact from the drop position. However, many players fail to achieve a complete drop, reducing the role of this fundamental factor. As any teaching pro knows, an incomplete drop is one of the most difficult flaws to correct. If this has been your problem, working with this key can eliminate it from your game. This key is also highly effective for players who may tend to shorten the motion under the pressure of match play. The key is shown from the player's perspective, the angle you will actually see it from in your own mind when you construct your mental image.

Note that the edge of the racket is in line with the center of the spine. The tip of the racket points down at the court, and the elbow position is high. Establish the Racket Drop physically. Now create the mental image. Test the key in controlled drill.

Keying the Basic Serve: The Contact Point from the Player's Perspective

○ ○ ○ ○ ○ ○ ○ ○ ○ ○ ○ ○ ○ ○ ○ ○ ○ ○ ○

High contact is crucial to the service motion. It ensures maximum net clearance; it also imparts the correct trajectory so that the ball lands consistently within the service box. High contact also maximizes body leverage, and is a major factor in shot velocity. The great servers are extended at contact from the tip of the toes to the tip of the racket. This key, presented from the player's perspective, is designed to help you achieve this yourself.

Note several key points: the arm is fully extended; it is directly above the shoulder; and the face of the racket is in front of the plane of the body, so that the contact is slightly out over the court. Establish the position physically and create the mental image.

Keying the Basic Serve: The Finish Position from the Player's Perspective

○ ○ ○ ○ ○ ○ ○ ○ ○ ○ ○ ○ ○ ○ ○ ○ ○

As with the groundstrokes, the followthrough on the serve is a primary key to maintaining racket head acceleration throughout the course of the stroke. A common tendency is to overhit the ball by tightening up the arm muscles. This leads to a short, constricted followthrough, and a loss of shot velocity, instead of a gain.

If you find that your followthrough is consistently short, this should be a primary key for you. At the end of the motion, your racket hand should touch down on your left front leg, as shown above. This full finish will allow you to keep the arm relaxed and the swing flowing. Establish the position physically and create the mental image. Now test the key in controlled drill. Hold the image at the correct finish, and make your hand and racket overlap this blueprint.

Keying the Basic Serve:
The Tossing Motion

○ ○ ○ ○ ○ ○ ○ ○ ○ ○ ○ ○ ○ ○ ○ ○ ○ ○

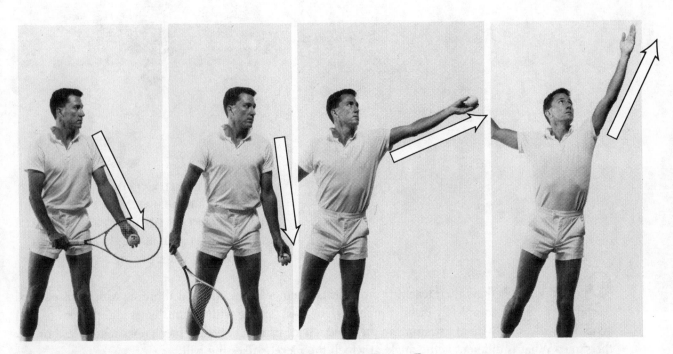

THIS SEQUENCE SHOWS THE STRAIGHT ARM POSITION AT THE READY POSITION, THE DROP OF THE ARMS, THE RELEASE OF THE BALL, AND THE EXTENSION OF THE MOTION.

Even if a player develops consistent muscle memory for the service motion, his delivery will be ineffective without a reliable toss. The key to the toss is to simplify it as much as possible. This means keeping the arm straight throughout the motion. Notice that with the arm locked at the elbow and the wrist there is no internal movement. Instead, the entire arm simply drops straight down from the hinge of the shoulder and then moves straight up to the ball release and full extension. Instead of throwing, or flipping the ball, the player simply opens his hand, allowing the ball to roll off of his fingertips. Thus, the ball toss is really more a ball *release*, rather than a toss or a throw. Typically, it is bending at the elbow or flipping the wrist that causes inconsistency in the toss placement. Execute the tossing motion with the arm straight several times. As you do, create a mental image. Now test the key in controlled drill. As you start the motion, visualize the image of your arm moving straight down and all the way up to the full extension.

Keying the Basic Serve: Developing Spin

○ ○ ○ ○ ○ ○ ○ ○ ○ ○ ○ ○ ○ ○ ○ ○ ○ ○

TO CREATE BALL ROTATION, THE RACKET
MUST STRIKE THE BALL AT A POINT TO THE
LOWER LEFT OF THE CENTER OF THE FACE
OF THE BALL AND MOVE ON A DIAGONAL
ACROSS THE FACE OF THE BALL.

Often, students will ask their teaching pro to teach them a "spin serve," as if hitting with spin required learning a new and completely distinct motion. However, hitting with various types and degrees of spin actually involves only slight variations in the basic service pattern. The bio-mechanics remain essentially the same. What is different is the angle at which the racket strikes the ball.

The first step in generating ball rotation is to change to the continental grip. If you bring your racket up to the Contact Point with the continental grip, you will see that the racket face will strike the ball at an angle. Many players who execute their basic service motion with the continental grip produce spin immediately and automatically. Initially, however, you may find that the ball moves too sharply to the left. To straighten it out you must learn to strike the ball at a point to the lower left of the center, with the racket face moving upward and across the face of the ball on a diagonal line, as shown below.

To create this image, close your eyes and imagine the path of the racket and the point of contact on the ball's surface. There are the two elements in the image—the diagonal path of the racket, and the spot to the lower left at which the racket contacts the ball. You may see it in terms of a still frame of the Contact Point, or a mini-movie of the racket as it moves through the swing. Test the image you create in controlled drill.

The additional ball rotation should give the flight of your serve a noticeable arc, and cause it to drop more sharply down into the serving box. This allows you to hit the serve with confidence and

202

pace, knowing that the ball rotation will keep it in the court. Once you feel comfortable with hitting spin in controlled drill, move on to practice points, and then match play.

At this point, you can begin to vary the type and the amount of rotation. Typically, by using the key shown above, a player will produce a ball that moves slightly from right to left, but one that also kicks up at least somewhat after the bounce. Most spin serves fall somewhere between pure slice, or a ball that rotates sideways from right to left, and pure topspin, or a ball that rotates from top to bottom. The ball spins at the angle of the diagonal at which the racket head is moving at contact.

As you develop your own particular serving style, you can experiment with variations on this basic spin. By altering the path of the diagonal line so that it is slightly more horizontal, you can generate more slice. This serve will have less arc, but will move more sharply from right to left. By making the diagonal slightly more vertical, you can generate more topspin. This serve will have more arc, and will travel in a straighter line, but it will also kick up much higher after the bounce.

A final factor influencing the type and amount of ball rotation is the placement of the toss. As described in the tossing key, a player should strive to place the toss directly above the hitting shoulder so that he can achieve maximum extension at contact. However, many players find that varying the toss placement by a few inches to the left or right makes it easier to achieve different spins. A toss slightly to the right of the shoulder increases the tendency to hit around the ball, generating slice. Similarly, a toss slightly back and to the left lends itself to hitting up and over the ball, generating topspin.

The bottom line is that most players gravitate to one type of rotation or the other. It is a question of determining which variation of toss and ball rotation is most natural and effective for you. However, after a period of experimentation, it is important that a player settle on one tossing variation.

The most effective approach, as noted at the beginning of the chapter, is to develop one basic type of ball rotation, and then to develop slight variations on that basic pattern based on the use of a single toss. This is in fact the usual pattern at the highest levels of pro tennis. John McEnroe, for example, hits the ball with a degree of sideways, slicing rotation. This is perfectly suited to his game and helps him move the ball around the service box as widely as possible. His toss, typical for this type of spin, is directly above his shoulder, or slightly to the right. Within this framework, McEnroe hits two additional variations: he can flatten out the delivery on his first serve, and he can increase the amount of spin as well, usually for his second delivery.

In contrast, players such as Ivan Lendl, Stefan Edberg, and Boris Becker serve with more of a topspin, kicking rotation. All three toss the ball more to the left than McEnroe—somewhere between the shoulder and the edge of the head. This tossing position is naturally conducive to hitting up and over the ball. It allows them to hit with more velocity, and is suited to their powerful styles. Like McEnroe, however, they have three basic variations on a single theme: a relatively flat first serve, a first serve hit with moderate rotation, and a second serve hit with increased spin. These three serves are mixed together as part of an overall serving strategy, depending on the opponent, the court surface, and the situation in a particular match.

Variation:
The Advanced Serve

○ ○ ○ ○ ○ ○ ○ ○ ○ ○ ○ ○ ○ ○ ○ ○

1	2	3	4	5
READY POSITION	**ARM DROP**	**START OF KNEE BEND**	**MAXIMUM BEND**	**START OF RELEASE**

Progression to the Advanced Serve: As noted in the introduction to this chapter, most of the great servers in the modern game use the advanced footwork shown here, which is also known as the thrust, or the hop. Every player who wishes to develop his serving ability to the fullest should eventually progress to the advanced serve shown above, but only after the bio-mechanics for the basic service motion are solid. This basic competence should include the ability to hit spin consistently on both the first and second serves.

Differences from Basic Serve: The distinguishing characteristic of the advanced serve is the greatly increased role of the legs in generating additional power and spin. A key element in the basic service motion is the weight shift forward to the front, left foot, and the accompanying knee bend. In the advanced serve, this weight shift and the knee bend are maximized (Frame 4). The result is that, as the motion uncoils, the player is literally propelled upward into the ball (Frame 7). This full use of the legs creates tremendous additional ball leverage, and can increase the velocity and ball rotation of your serve by as much as 25 percent.

Producing the Advanced Serve: The key element in creating the advanced serve is increasing the knee bend at the beginning of the motion, starting when the arms drop (Frame 2), and continuing until the bend is maximized at the completion of the Backswing (Frame 4). By going down in the knees as far as possible, the player guarantees that he will uncoil upward into the ball as an

6	7	8	9	10	11
RACKET DROP	START OF KICK	CONTACT POINT	FOLLOWTHROUGH	LAND ON LEFT FOOT	FINISH POSITION

automatic consequence of the hitting motion (Frames 6 through 8). As the legs release upward into the ball the player simultaneously kicks his rear foot back and away from his body (Frames 8 through 11). The rear foot serves as a counterweight, allowing the player to launch himself upward into the ball, while remaining on balance and straight up and down at the waist. Aside from this greatly increased roll of the legs, the bio-mechanics of the motion are unchanged, and all the stroke keys from the basic serve apply.

Landing on the Front Foot: A central aspect of the advanced footwork is that the player lands on his left, front foot (Frame 10). Thus at the conclusion of the motion, the right foot is still behind, as it has been through the motion. He has not stepped forward and through the shot—in fact, the back leg has actually moved *away* from his body, kicking backward as the motion uncoils. This relationship between the feet is crucial for unlocking the added power of the legs, and retaining the proper sequence of the body rotation into the ball. If a player is proceding to net, he can then take the next step forward with the back leg, or he can simply recover to the Ready Position for baseline play. In developing this motion it is important to be able to stop the motion and retain balance after the hop, with the weight still on the front foot (Frame 11).

Keying the Advanced Serve: Maximizing Knee Bend

○ ○ ○ ○ ○ ○ ○ ○ ○ ○ ○ ○ ○

IMAGE OF MAXIMUM KNEE BEND
WITH THE WEIGHT SHIFTED FULLY
FORWARD TO THE FRONT FOOT.

The use of the legs in the advanced serve motion preserves and expands upon the bio-mechanics of the basic motion. The basic serve calls for a shift of the weight to the left foot, knee bend, with the right foot finishing up on the tips of the toes. The advanced serve takes this basic leg action to its logical conclusion. By adding this increased knee bend the player can generate significant additional velocity and spin, without any other changes in the motion, and he can continue to use the full range of keys developed for the basic serve in executing the advanced motion. These keys are supplemented by the knee bend key shown above.

The first step in developing the knee bend key is determining physically how far down you are capable of bending. This will depend on your physical strength, and also, your flexibility. Players such as McEnroe go down until the knees are bent almost at a right angle. Most players cannot match this, but this is something you must determine for yourself. The bend shown above is a fairly typical maximum for most players. To do this, let the arm drop and start the knee bend. Shift as much weight as possible to the left front foot and see how far down in the knees you can actually go. Now create the visual image, as shown above. See yourself from the waist down with your weight on the left, front foot, and the maximum possible bend. As you start your service motion, hold the image of your knee bend, and make your legs overlap the image. Visualize yourself staying down as long as possible. As the swing progresses, you will automatically uncoil upward from the legs. You should land on your front foot, with the rear leg kicking backward, as described below. Now test the key in controlled drill.

Keying the Advanced Serve: Kicking Back with the Back Leg

○ ○ ○ ○ ○ ○ ○ ○ ○ ○ ○ ○ ○ ○

THIS IMAGE SHOWS HOW THE BACK
RIGHT LEG SERVES AS A COUNTER-
WEIGHT, KICKING AWAY FROM
THE BODY AS THE MOTION UNCOILS.

As noted in the introduction to this chapter, probably the most common flaw in most service motions is the tendency to step through the motion with the back leg. This throws off the synchronization of the motion, makes the body rotation too early, causes a loss of power, and is responsible for much of the serving inconsistency in the modern game, even at the highest levels of professional tennis.

This key is designed to help you control the back foot properly, and is crucial to the proper use of the legs on the advanced serve. By kicking out and away from the body as the knees uncoil, the back leg serves as a counterweight. It allows the player to retain good balance, remain straight up and down from the waist, and also, achieve full extension at contact. Most important, the leg kick keeps the player's weight behind the ball, so he can take full advantage of the extra body leverage generated by the uncoiling of the legs, and still land on the front foot, as demonstrated in the sequence photos of the advanced serve. If you watch the great serve and volley players you will see that they almost all land on the front foot, before continuing on to the net. This is possible only if the rear leg is used correctly for balance.

To create this key, start in the Ready Position. Now drop the arms and bend the knees, going down to whatever is your maximum amount of bend. Then, without continuing the swing or hitting the ball, release the knees so that you hop upward and forward. As you do this, kick your rear, right leg back and away from your body as shown above. Now, repeat this motion, and create a visual image of the right leg as it moves backward. Test the key in controlled drill. Once the advanced footwork is solid, you can alternate the key for kicking back and for the increased knee bend with the other keys that are active for your particular service motion, such as the Toss, the Racket Drop, etc.

USING YOUR STROKE KEYS ON THE COURT

By following the progressions in the individual chapters, you have developed models and keys for each of the individual strokes. You should now have a clear mental picture of every aspect of your game. If used correctly this system of keys provides a method for achieving superior execution on a regular basis. To do this, however, means having the mental discipline to think about what you are doing when you are actually on the court. Playing consistently excellent tennis requires consistently excellent mental focus. In my opinion, this is rarely achieved below the highest levels of the game. Many, if not most, players allow their minds to wander wildly during match play. Their thoughts are dominated by fears about choking or losing the match, or worse, they drift away to entirely unrelated subjects. The stroke key system is designed to eliminate this tendency, by giving you a clear framework for blocking out fears and other distracting thoughts on the court and creating continuous mental focus. This ability is crucial if you want to achieve your goals in the game of tennis.

It does no good to do the development work in lessons and controlled drill if the player never truly applies what he has learned in his matches. For many players, doing this requires radically changing their mental patterns. From the moment you walk on the court until the completion of match point, you should use the keying process described in the preceding chapters. This means knowing what your active keys are for every stroke, visualizing them beginning with the start of the warm-up, and continuing this process unbroken through the course of the match.

Often, players who are struggling to develop this mental framework do best by actually taking stroke key charts on the court with them. The stroke charts are a physical reminder of how the player intends to think during the match, and they are a reference source that the player can consult on the game change-overs. For example, if your backhand becomes erratic, you can use your backhand stroke key chart to remind yourself what your tendencies are, identify the problem, and apply the counteracting key. A player who truly reshapes his mental approach using the visual system presented here has the tools for reaching whatever goals he sets for himself in tennis.

Following are examples of stroke key charts constructed by two of my students. They can serve as models for creating charts of your own. There is also a blank chart that you can Xerox in order to do this.

The stroke key chart included here allows you to deal with any situation that may occur on the court. It is divided into two parts: keys and tendency analysis. For each stroke you should develop a series of two to four primary keys. When you go to the court, begin the warm-up by consciously visualizing one or more of these keys to activate your stroke. From this point on, the goal is to hold a specific key image on every shot throughout the match.

The second part of the chart is tendency analysis. Typically, when a stroke breaks down, it will be one of a limited number of elements that are incorrect. Every player has his tendencies, the way he happens to deviate from the model strokes. The art is in identifying what your particular tendencies are, and how to manage them on the court. The beauty of doing tendency analysis is that it allows you to correct your errors as they happen. By working in controlled drill, and by doing video and match play analysis with a teaching pro or coach, each player should pinpoint the tendencies in each of his strokes that lead to technical breakdowns and unforced errors. Then each tendency should be paired with one more counteracting key. Because each player will have only a limited number of tendencies, it is easy to identify the source of errors. The player is then pre-

pared to deal with any breakdowns in stroke production that occur in the course of play, and to correct them virtually instantaneously.

For example, against a hard-hitting opponent, a player may tend to feel rushed and fail to achieve complete preparation. The counteracting key is to visualize the image of the correct racket and shoulder position at the Turn. Then as the motion starts, the player simply makes his racket and shoulder position overlap the image, and his preparation problem is eliminated. Or against a weaker opponent, a player may overhit the ball trying to win the points too quickly, shortening the followthrough and hitting long. The counteracting key here should be some variation on the image of the Finish Position. By visualizing the correct position of the racket on the followthrough, and then bringing his racket to this image, the player can eliminate the tendency to constrict the swing and muscle the ball, quickly reestablishing a full, fluid stroke pattern.

The stroke keys provide an almost foolproof system for executing your strokes with consistent technical excellence, and if your stroke execution is consistently excellent, you will play your best tennis on a regular basis, and win more than your share of matches. This will happen because you will eliminate unforced errors from your game, the major problem faced by all players below the professional level. Your matches will then be won or lost by superior shot making. This ability to hit your shots under pressure will take your game to a higher level than you may have thought possible. By using your stroke keys on the big points, you can go for the execution of your shots, and let the chips fall where they may, knowing that more often than not, you will make the shot if your swing simply follows the model stroke.

If you use your personal stroke keys correctly and consistently, you will experience the physical and aesthetic pleasure of playing technically superior, classical tennis. Playing tennis with this level of skill and confidence can be phenomenally satisfying. I think you will find that it is more than worth the effort required.

PERSONAL STROKE KEY CHART

NAME: _Sara Welch_ AGE: _17_

ABILITY LEVEL: _Girl's 18's Ranked Junior_

STROKE: _2-Handed Backhand_

ACTIVE KEYS:
1. _Image of smooth stroke_
2. _Hit up on ball_
3. _Set on front foot_
4. _____

TENDENCIES:

TENDENCY:	KEY:
releasing wrist	Wrist back at finish
hitting long	hit up on ball

PERSONAL STROKE KEY CHART

NAME: _CLIFF WEST_____ AGE: __41_____

ABILITY LEVEL: __A_____

STROKE: __FOREHAND GROUNDSTROKE_____

ACTIVE KEYS: 1. __IMAGE OF TURN_____

2. __WRIST BACK / VERTICAL SWING____

3. __WEIGHT ON FRONT FOOT_____

4. __FULL KNEE BEND_____

TENDENCIES:

TENDENCY:	KEY:
HIT SHORT	EARLY CONTACT
HIT LONG	HIT UP AT CONTACT

PERSONAL STROKE KEY CHART

NAME:_ AGE:_ _ _ _ _ _ _ _ _ _ _ _ _ _ _

ABILITY LEVEL:_ _

STROKE:_ _

ACTIVE KEYS: 1._ _

                 2._ _

                 3._ _

                 4._ _

TENDENCIES:

TENDENCY: KEY:

_ _ _ _ _ _ _ _ _ _ _ _ _ _ _ _ _   _ _ _ _ _ _ _ _ _ _ _ _ _ _ _ _ _

_ _ _ _ _ _ _ _ _ _ _ _ _ _ _ _ _   _ _ _ _ _ _ _ _ _ _ _ _ _ _ _ _ _

_ _ _ _ _ _ _ _ _ _ _ _ _ _ _ _ _   _ _ _ _ _ _ _ _ _ _ _ _ _ _ _ _ _

THE GRIPS

T he foundation for developing each of the classical stroke patterns is the correct grip. As previously discussed, most players already have some version of the correct grip on most strokes. However, if you have questions about your grip, or about the possible grip variations on a given stroke, this chapter should answer them.

The terminology used to define the various grip positions has varied over the years. There are many points of confusion, stemming from the way the grips have changed in the evolution of the modern game.[1]

On the forehand, I have outlined two variations—the pure eastern, and the modified eastern. While most authorities agree with my definition of the pure eastern grip, others would call what I label the modified eastern the "extreme eastern" or even the "semi-western." In my opinion, however, this grip is a relatively slight modification of the pure eastern grip and is central to classical stroke production. Far from being "extreme," it is the grip that the majority of players find most comfortable and effective. Although this grip rotates the palm slightly downward toward the western position, the term "semi-western" is still inappropriate, since this grip is commonly used to produce a classical swing pattern. The term "semi-western" implies that the swing will have some of the characteristics of the western game, which is untrue. Even a player such as Andre Agassi, who pushes the modified eastern grip further toward the western than most players, plays with

---

[1]*For the best discussion of the grips, using the older terminology, see Paul Metzler,* Tennis Styles and Stylists *(New York: Macmillan, 1969), pp. 201–8.*

what is best described as a classical technical style.

In defining the backhand grips, there is also considerable confusion. Some writers would call the eastern backhand grip described here "continental," since two great champions of the past, Fred Perry and Rod Laver, played with this grip on both the forehand and backhand. According to this viewpoint, a "true" eastern backhand grip would be the more extreme heavy topspin grip discussed below. What I have called the eastern backhand grip is, however, the grip used almost universally by the eastern-style players discussed in this book, and thus, in discussing the modern game, it makes the most sense to label it as such.

What I have called the continental grip is the grip used by most players on both the volley and the serve, falling halfway in between the eastern forehand and the eastern backhand. This grip is sometimes called the "Australian," or the "modified continental." I refer to it as simply the continental, since it is the grip that is most commonly used on the serve and on the volleys by classical players. It is, in fact, the grip used on every stroke by John McEnroe, one of the very few pure continental stylists in the modern era.

Finally, it is important to note that, when it comes to defining the position of the hand on the racket for the various grips, I have abandoned the traditional alignment of the "V" formed by the thumb and forefinger as the main check-point. Instead, throughout this chapter, I have used the position of the lower heel pad of the racket hand. This is a change that has been long overdue in the theory of tennis instruction.

Because the shape and proportions of people's hands vary so much, the same "V" alignment can produce different grips with different players, even if the player is using the correct grip size. But more significant still is the change in the shape of racket handles with the introduction of the oversize and mid-size graphite and synthetic frames. Because of the slimness of the new racket shafts, the handles are now much more rectangular than the old wooden frames which were used to devise the "V" checkpoints. For example, on the eastern forehand grip, the traditional check-point is to align the "V" in the center of the top racket bevel. As the photos clearly show, however, using a modern frame, the "V" is to the right of center, with the pure eastern grip. And on the most common eastern forehand grip, the modified eastern, it is off the top bevel altogether.

If you have been hitting your forehand with a grip based on the alignment of the "V," you may actually be trying to hit your forehand with some version of a backhand grip. In any case, the alignment of the heel pad gives a much more accurate indication of the position of the palm in relation to the racket head, which is the central factor in achieving a correct grip for any stroke.

THE FOREHAND GRIPS

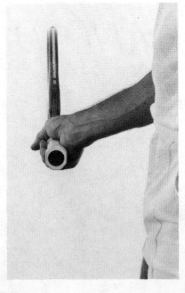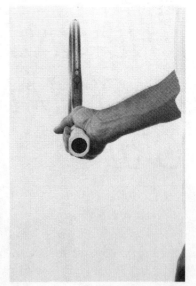

THE PURE EASTERN GRIP. THE HEEL PADS AT THE EDGE OF THE TOP BEVEL OF THE RACKET HANDLE. (LEFT)   THE MODIFIED EASTERN FOREHAND GRIP, THE MORE COMMON AND EFFECTIVE VERSION OF THE CLASSICAL FOREHAND GRIP. NOTE THE SLIGHTLY LOWER HEEL PAD POSITION. (RIGHT)

The central characteristic of the classical or eastern forehand grip is that it places the palm of the hand in line with the face of the racket. This means that when the hand is closed around the racket, most of the palm is on the *back* bevel of the handle. This palm position allows the player to hit through the shot with the wrist slightly laid back, without releasing it at contact. A correct forehand grip, then, is critical to the proper execution of the stroke.

To get the forehand grip, hold the racket by the throat with your *left* hand. Place your *right* palm flat on the face of the strings and simply slide your palm down along the shaft of the racket to the grip. Now close your hand around the grip and shake hands with the racket. The top, index finger should be slightly spread from the rest of the fingers.

The key checkpoint in determining whether the grip is correct is the position of the heel pad of the hand. It should be on either the top or middle side bevel of the handle. If any part of the heel pad is on the *top* bevel of the frame, you no longer have an eastern forehand grip. Instead, you have some version of a backhand or continental grip. To correct this, simply rotate your hand slightly to the right to reposition the heel pad.

Within this general framework, there are two major variations of the forehand grip. They will work equally well in producing the classical stroke. Which you chose is really a matter of comfort and preference. If the heel pad is on the top *side* bevel (see forehand photos), then this is a "pure" eastern forehand grip. The heel pad is as close as possible to the top of the frame, without actually touching the top bevel. This grip is used by players such as Chris Evert and Martina Navratilova.

The second variation is the modified eastern forehand grip. In this grip, the hand has rotated slightly further to the right, so that the heel pad is resting on the center, *back* bevel of the racket handle. This is the grip used by Ivan Lendl, Steffi Graf, and Jimmy Connors, among many others. It is probably the predominant forehand grip in recreational and tournament tennis today, and most players find it more comfortable than the pure eastern version.

THE ONE-HANDED BACKHAND GRIP

THE EASTERN BACKHAND GRIP. THE HEEL PAD HAS ROTATED TO THE LEFT OF THE FOREHAND AND IS ON THE TOP BEVEL OF THE FRAME.

To hit the one-handed backhand, it is necessary to change the grip at the beginning of the stroke. To do this, rotate your racket hand to the left, toward the *top* of the frame, until your heel pad is resting squarely on the top bevel. The second, lower knuckle of the index finger should now be in line with the center of the top *right* bevel.

The eastern backhand grip will work equally well for hitting the ball flat, with topspin, or with slice. There are two other possible one-hand backhand grips, although in my opinion, neither one is advisable for developing classical stroke patterns. The first is an extreme eastern backhand grip, in which the hand is rotated even further to the left. This grip will produce heavier topspin on the backhand, but forces the player to make contact much further in front of the body is very difficult to time. Also, it is much tougher to hit a solid slice backhand using this grip, since it is necessary to dip the swing radically under the ball, to make contact with an open racket face. Doing this requires movement in the elbow and the wrist, and is a major source of potential errors. Using this grip, the player simply cannot hit through the ball on a line to produce slice, as demonstrated in the backhand chapter.

The other alternative backhand grip is the continental—the same grip shown in this chapter for use on the serve and volleys. This grip places *part* of the heel pad on the top bevel, but the heel pad does not sit squarely on the top of the frame. Although this grip is probably equal, or even slightly superior, to the eastern backhand for hitting the slice drive, it is more difficult to generate topspin using it. To hit topspin, it is necessary to tilt the wrist downward to get the racket face vertical at contact, and this results in a loss of body leverage, somewhat later contact, and a tendency to have too much internal arm movement. Since a good one-handed player needs to hit both with equal facility, the eastern backhand grip is clearly the best choice for the majority of players.

THE TWO-HANDED BACKHAND GRIP

THE TWO-HANDED BACKHAND GRIP, WHICH IS ACTUALLY TWO FOREHAND GRIPS, EACH WITH THE SAME HEEL PAD POSITION. (LEFT)   THE TWO-HANDED GRIP VARIATION SHOWING THE EASTERN BACKHAND GRIP WITH THE RIGHT HAND. (RIGHT)

The correct grip for the two-handed backhand is essentially *two* eastern forehand grips, one with each hand. Start with your forehand grip with your right hand (whether pure or modified eastern). Now place the *left* hand on the face of the strings, and slide it down along the shaft of the racket and onto the grip, until your hands are touching. Close the fingers of your left hand around the racket handle. You should now have a forehand grip with each hand.

As is the case with the right hand forehand grip, the grip with the left hand can be either a pure eastern, or a modified eastern. The purpose is to put the palm of the left hand in line with the face of the racket. Again, most players will probably be more comfortable with the modified version, but you may want to experiment for yourself.

As discussed in the backhand chapter, an advanced variation on the two-handed stroke is the addition of a complimentary one-handed slice backhand, as developed by players such as Bjorn Borg and Mats Wilander. To do this requires changing the grip with the *right* hand to an eastern backhand. A player with a two-hand backhand who is learning to hit slice should wait in the Ready Position with both forehand grips. When he starts the turn, he then simply rotates the right hand toward the top of the handle to the eastern backhand grip position, as he would if he were a one-handed player. The grip with the left hand should remain unchanged. At this point, he then has the option of hitting the two-handed backhand, which is dominated by the left arm and shoulder, or of letting go with the left hand, and hitting the slice using the bio-mechanics of the one-handed shot. If he stays with the two-handed shot, the change in grip with the right hand will have no significant impact on the stroke—it simply prepares him to hold the racket correctly if he chooses instead to hit the slice. As explained in the text, however, this transition back between the two-handed and the one-handed slice backhands is a difficult one, and should be developed only by advanced players once the two-handed shot is fundamentally sound and reliable in match play.

THE CONTINENTAL GRIP

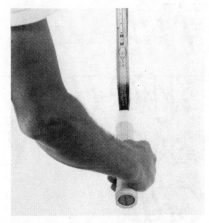

THE CONTINENTAL GRIP, WITH THE HEEL PAD POSITIONED BETWEEN THE EASTERN FOREHAND AND THE EASTERN BACKHAND GRIPS.

As described in the discussion of backhand grips, the continental grip is approximately halfway between the pure eastern forehand, and the eastern backhand. This means that the heel pad of the racket hand is *partially* on top of the top bevel of the racket frame. This is the ideal grip for hitting spin on the volleys and on the serve.

On the volley, it allows a player to come under the ball with natural underspin, without having to distort the stroke pattern. With the classical forehand grip, in comparison, this is impossible without using the wrist and dipping the racket head under the ball, particularly on low volleys where hitting with underspin is essential. There is a similar, though less severe, dipping action required to hit a slice on the backhand volley with the classical eastern backhand grip. By comparison, the continental grip will produce underspin automatically on both volleys, without the need to alter the path of the racket head. It also has the advantage of allowing the player to volley on both sides without having to change grips.

As discussed in the volley chapter, it is important first to learn the volleys with the same grips as the groundstrokes, and initially to hit the ball flat, until the bio-mechanics of the motion are solid. Only then should the player experiment with the continental grip. Some players never get comfortable with the continental grip on the forehand volley, and others find it becomes natural quite quickly. This is not a clear-cut choice and every player should make this decision on the basis of his own experimentation. Two-handed volleyers face basically the same choice, but only on the forehand volley, since there is no grip change necessary to hit the two-handed backhand volley.

On the serve, using either the continental, or the eastern backhand grip is essential to generating spin, a basic aspect of effective serving. By changing the grip to one of these variations, the server will automatically produce ball rotation since the grip change will alter the angle at which the racket face strikes the ball.

For the majority of players, this brushing action will feel more natural with the continental grip. The continental grip is a less radical change from the forehand grip, which is used in learning the basic serve. The eastern backhand is somewhat more awkward for most players to learn. Using the eastern grip, he is likely to hit too much around the side of the ball, generating excessive slice, and losing pace. In order to make really solid contact with this grip, the player must also learn to radically pronate his forearm outward as it comes up toward the ball. With the continental grip, the spin is developed more naturally within the context of the exact swing pattern used on the basic serve.